Get the Most Out of Life

Get the Most Out of Life
Copyright ©2003 by Derrick Sweet

We acknowledge the financial support of the Government of Canada through the Book Publishing Industry Development Program for our publishing activities.

ISBN: 1-894622-38-3

Published by Warwick Publishing Inc.
161 Frederick Street, Toronto, Ontario M5A 4P3 Canada
www.warwickgp.com

Distributed in Canada by
Canadian Book Network
c/o Georgetown Terminal Warehouses
34 Armstrong Avenue
Georgetown, Ontario L7G 4R9

Distributed in the United States by
Weatherhill
41 Monroe Turnpike
Turnbull, Connecticut 06611 U.S.A.

Editor: Jennifer Iveson
Cover: Clint Rogerson
Layout: Melinda Tate
Printed and bound in Canada

Get the Mst Out of Life

Derrick Sweet

W

Warwick Publishing

Dedication

I dedicate this book to you, the reader. I dedicate this book to all the people in the world who still believe in their higher self and their unlimited potential, especially those of you who are committed to the journey to find these within yourselves. I dedicate this book to those of you who are having a tough time for one reason or another. Perhaps someone who cares about you thought the ideas in this book could help. They will.

Almost 25 years ago two desperate parents gave Dr. Wayne Dyer's book *The Sky's the Limit* to their teenage son. Their son was a high school drop-out, a constant worry, and a challenge, to say the least. He had no confidence, no hope, and no ambition. His parents were hoping for a miracle. I dedicate this book to my parents, Betty and Ray Sweet, who never gave up on "what was possible," and for seeing my higher self when no one else did — especially me! You two are the best living examples of unconditional love and support that I have ever known!

And finally, I dedicate this book to my mentor, Dr. Wayne Dyer, who for more than 30 years has been making a significant contribution to the lives of millions of people throughout the world through his books, recordings, and lectures. At the time of this writing, Dr. Dyer continues to write and lecture on the topics of human potential, spiritual connection, and living life to the fullest. Dr. Dyer: you are a miracle!

Contents

Section 3:
The Search for the Higher Self

Section 4: Golden Rules

Section 5: Keeping the Balance

Section 6: Last Remarks

Acknowledgements

There are so many people I would like to recognize for their input, support, and guidance in the development of this book.

First and foremost, I would like to thank my publisher, Warwick Publishing, for its interest in the ideas behind this book. I am especially grateful for the sincere enthusiasm of Nick Pitt, at Warwick, who embraced this project from the beginning. Appreciation goes, as well, to my editor Jennifer Iveson for her mastery of the written word.

To my wife Marsha for her willingness to listen and re-listen and yet re-listen again to all the ideas in this book: your feedback, thoughts, and enthusiasm keep me moving in the right direction. To my good friends and advisors, Gino Ciavarella, Jonas and Catherine Friel, and Gordon Corbett: I am truly blessed to have your friendship and support.

To my business associate David Aaron, who runs the day-to-day affairs of the Healthy Wealthy and Wise Corporation: your dedication, enthusiasm, and relentless persistence are an inspiration. Thank you!

To Richard Dolan, Michael Holmes, Howard Gross, David McBain, Udaya Ratnayake, Ajay Dhebar, David Sersta, and Frank Cianchetti: your belief in me, your guidance, and your faith gave me the strength to "dig deep" to write this book.

I thank the speakers' bureaus across the United States

and Canada who continue to support the message of this book by recommending my keynote presentations to their most trusted clients.

To our corporate clients, especially Mike Matthew, Eva Durnford, Paul Leblanc, Irene Klatt, Michel Losier, Lise Bujold, Denis Empringham, and Francois Duguay, who repeatedly invite me to speak to your organizations: you are all ambassadors of the powerful message in this book.

And finally to my parents, Betty and Ray Sweet: your support, love, and unimaginable belief in me have always been the octane in my tank, the spring in my step, the passion in my eyes, and the fire in my belly. I have always and will always feel your collective spirit in everything I do! You have taught me, more than anyone, how to Get the Most Out of Life — for this I am, and will always be, truly grateful!

Introduction

For the last 20 years, I have been researching one simple theme: getting the most out of life. Great thinkers like Buddha, Marcus Aurelius, Leonardo Da Vinci, and Charles Darwin exposed many of the consistent habits, actions, and "ways of thinking" to live life to the fullest.

The last two hundred years, especially, have been very exciting in the world of human potential. Just look at great minds and leaders like Helen Keller, Ralph Waldo Emerson, Albert Einstein, Abraham Lincoln, Sigmund Freud, Mahatma Gandhi, and Eleanor Roosevelt, to name a few. They have all made significant contributions to shedding light not only on how to get the most out of life, but also on why so many people give up before they've become what they're truly capable of becoming.

What you'll discover in the following pages may not necessarily be new — in fact, most of it is thousands of years old. You might say, in fact, that what you'll read in this book is just common sense. Unfortunately, what may be considered "common sense" is seldom commonly practiced. The one constant in the past several thousand years is that people are always searching but rarely finding lasting peace, joy, and abundance. Everyone wants to be happy, kind, helpful, courteous, and loving; however, most people are going about it the wrong way. Most people seem to have an ongoing internal struggle between negative thoughts and positive thoughts. The information in this book will reveal why people have these internal struggles.

The book will also teach you how to avoid falling into the common traps and illusions that would otherwise prevent you from living to your fullest potential.

To get the most out of this book, you'll need to read it with a journal or notebook by your side. You should also start at the beginning of the book, instead of skipping around; each page gives you information you may need to fully understand future pages. You'll notice a few ideas that crop up in more than one section — this is not an accident. Pay attention to these! Their universality is their strength.

Periodically you'll be asked to answer a question or participate in an exercise that may ask you to write a few ideas down. These exercises are designed specifically for you. If you commit to giving a hundred per cent effort to reading and re-reading this book, doing the exercises, and answering the questions, your awareness of your true potential will be revealed. And I guarantee you that it is nothing short of awesome! The information you are about to discover will change the way you see yourself, your surroundings, and your future; it will give you all the tools you need to get the most out of life!

Good luck!

Derrick Sweet

Section 1
The Big Idea

Develop Patience

Patience serves as a protection against wrongs as clothes do against cold. For if you put on more clothes as the cold increases, it will have no power to hurt you. So in like manner you must grow in patience when you meet with great wrongs, and they will be powerless to vex your mind.
—Leonardo Da Vinci, Italian sculptor, painter, and architect

WE LIVE IN A WORLD today that wants and expects instant everything.

We are a society that has no time to waste. Take the television remote control, affectionately known in many homes as the zapper, for example. We can't even watch a one-hour program without seeing what else is on during the commercials.

And forget about wasting all that time cooking. Slowly the sit-down meal is becoming extinct. Instead, meal-replacement bars, microwaveables, and take-out rule.

If our marriage is going through a rough patch (and what marriage doesn't?), our impatience finds an outlet in the instant divorce. In traffic we have zero tolerance for anyone who hesitates or drives slower than we do. How easily and naturally we say: "Move it, you idiot!" without any consideration of the consequences of this type of behavior for our spirit. Why are we in such a hurry, anyway?

We all crave peace of mind, joy, and

abundance, but the problem is that we want it *now*. The wisdom and peace that we all desire can only be achieved through methodically, lovingly, and patiently persevering through life's lessons.

By writing in your journal the lessons of the day and periodically taking the time to reflect upon them, by practicing the discipline of daily meditation, by being in the moment — this is how wisdom is earned. Wisdom can't be purchased at a convenience store or on-line. There are no stores called "Wisdom-to-Go" and there is no such thing as a "wisdominator" for only three payments of $29.95.

There are no shortcuts to getting the most out of life! So, take a deep breath, kick off your shoes, and curl up with a good book.

Your Higher Self

WE ARE ALL BORN with a very powerful gift. Most people take this gift to the grave without realizing they even had it. We are all born with a higher self. Some people call this higher self "divinity," others call it "spirit." You may want to call it your "true self."

Your higher self is the part of you that sees the good in a situation, that wants to be at peace with the world. It doesn't judge, criticize, or condemn. Your higher self wants to make a significant contribution to the world, to serve a worthy purpose, and to spend its time in positive pursuits. Your higher self is the little voice you periodically hear saying, "What can I do right now to serve, to make someone's day, or to just help out?"

When you are functioning in the realm of your higher self you will develop an uncanny ability to focus on solutions rather than problems. To be happy, fulfilled, and at peace, you must learn to tune out the lower self and tune in the higher self.

That's how to get the most out of life, and that's what this book is about. There are lots of fun ways to tap into your higher self, like writing in a journal, meditating, and spending time with nature. You'll read more about these later in the book. You'll also find some exercises in here that will show you how to find, understand, and benefit from the power of your higher self.

3

Your Lower Self

ALL OF US WERE BORN with a lower self. This lower self is often referred to as the ego. It is your lower self's role to create a sense of self-worth that is defined by how different you are from everyone else.

The lower self is driven by emotions like greed and fear because of its focus on competition, judgment, comparison, and scarcity. Your lower self defines who you are by external measuring sticks like how much money you make, what you do for a living, what people say about you, and what part of town you live in. Your lower self is never at peace and is never satisfied.

The truth is, as long as we believe we are separate from everyone else, we will always experience a nagging feeling of isolation and emptiness, no matter how many material "goodies" we surround ourselves with. We all know people who live in this illusion.

Happiness, in the pure sense of the word, will always elude those who listen to the lower self. Your biggest challenge in life will be the ongoing battle to quiet the lower self and listen to the higher self. The lower self is relentless in its desire to dominate your thoughts.

But the good news is that you can silence the lower self, with time and a tenacious commitment to living in the realm of your higher self.

The first step is to learn how to tell the two selves apart. Any thought that weakens you, such as judgment, criticism, doubt, comparison, or fear, comes from the lower self. Just realizing that there is an alternative to this type of thinking will allow you to mute the lower self.

That's not to say that you'll never have thoughts that weaken you, because you will. These thoughts will surface periodically as a result of years of past conditioning. Your goal is this: Any time a weakening thought enters your consciousness, recognize its source, cancel it out, and then immediately replace it with a thought from your higher self.

This awareness and discipline will create incredible peace of mind in your life!

Understand Your Mind

A man is literally what he thinks.
—James Allen,
American essayist

*T*HE BELIEFS YOU HAVE about yourself, whether empowering or self-defeating, are being reinforced by your subconscious mind 24 hours a day. Yes, even in your dreams.

Have you ever said to yourself: "Why am I so out of shape?" or "How come I don't have more money saved for my retirement?" or "I always get nervous speaking in front of large groups." Each time you have these self-defeating thoughts, whether consciously or not, your mind "sees" you out of shape, broke, or shy.

This seeing can be conscious — like a daydream — or unconscious, meaning it's so automatic you don't even notice it. Either way, this image reinforces the original thought, creating a vicious cycle of negative thinking.

And your subconscious mind doesn't know the difference between reality and imagination. Think of your mind as a camera, where your conscious thoughts are the lens (that you choose to point at positive pictures or negative ones) and your subconscious is the film. Film is powerless: it has no choice but to develop an image of what it is pointed at, and cannot avoid being exposed if the button is pressed.

For example, if someone has thought of herself as fat and ugly for 10 years, those thoughts (the lens) are reinforced by a powerful mental image (the film). Then, say she loses 15 pounds, dyes her hair, and looks great. If she doesn't change her habit of functioning in the realm of her lower self, she will still look at herself in the mirror (or point her "lens") and say things like: "If I could just lose 10 more pounds!" or "Why is my skin so pale?" or "I hate the way my nose looks." And so, her subconscious (the "film") will continue to develop images produced by negative thinking, and her sense of self will not improve. (This explains why so many diets don't work.) What she has to do is stop the thought process in its tracks and change direction.

One of the reasons why most people are not getting the most out of life is that they allow any and all thoughts to enter their subconscious mind. Many of these unwanted thoughts come from images we take in while watching the evening news and television programs that feature "coarse language" and "scenes of violence." We've been conditioned to take it all in — without giving a second thought to the potential negative consequences for our subconscious mind, not to mention our spirit. The images that you consistently program into your subconscious mind will ultimately determine the outcome of your life.

So watch your thoughts and limit, or better yet, avoid images and thoughts that weaken you. Any time you have a self-defeating thought, recognize it as old, false programming and immediately replace it with a self-empowering one.

Remember the wise words of American writer Henry David Thoreau: "Thought is the sculptor who can create the person you want to be."

5

Understand Your Decisions

*O*UR LIFE IS A CONSTANT unfolding of cause and effect. In India, they call this karma. You are constantly making decisions (most of the time unconsciously) that determine your state of mind, financial health, physical well-being, and general outlook.

Sadly, most people unconsciously allow these decisions to be governed by outside stimuli like weather, media, culture, friends, family, and associates. In that scenario, it is only possible to *react* to the world; there is no hope for control.

People often say things they soon regret or, worse, do things they soon hope to forget. With this "reaction response," you have no power — only fear, doubt, and anxiety.

Being proactive, however, is to be in total control of your journey toward your desired outcome. The only way to be consistently proactive is to consciously think through every single decision you make. It sounds simple, and it is. But it's

27

very difficult to do. You must employ radar-type sensitivity to every thought you have.

Let's say you're in traffic and you get cut off. The reactionary response may be to send the driver in the other lane a not-so-kind gesture, followed by some not-so-nice words. This response, which is quite typical, is consistent with a reactionary (out of control) state of mind. It robs you of positive energy, peace of mind, and any kind of spiritual connection. It prevents you from feeling in control of yourself. That's not who you really are, it's definitely not your higher self, and it's not the person that you want to be.

A proactive response would be to stop and think, and then react in a way that is consistent with the vision of your higher self. After thinking (even for only a split second), your higher self may respond with an empowering thought like, "I'm so lucky that guy didn't scratch my car."

Again, this takes incredible discipline, but it leads to incredible destinations!

The Power of Belief

The man who believes he can do something is probably right, and so is the man who believes he can't.
—Oprah Winfrey, host of *The Oprah Winfrey Show* and businesswoman

*T*O BELIEVE IS TO ACCEPT something as truth. Whether what you believe is true or not has little influence on how your beliefs can influence your thoughts, attitudes, emotions, and actions.

Some people believe that Friday the 13th is bad luck. Others believe that carrying a dead rabbit's foot is good luck. Unfortunately, the beliefs of most people were programmed for them unconsciously, by their family and friends, their environment, and the media. As we have seen, these dominating beliefs program their actions.

It's a simple idea: what we do (our behavior) is a habit (or conditioned response) based on the belief system we have within us. So, if our unconscious beliefs are negative or limiting, our behavior will by definition be that way too.

Most of us, at one time or another, have had beliefs that limit us or hold us back. If you're shy around large groups of people, for example, it may be because of a limiting belief. Shyness really only exists if you believe you're shy. Maybe in junior high, you had a negative experience while giving a presentation to your class. Maybe you were nervous (a totally normal and expected feeling), and your teacher called that feeling "shyness." So you unconsciously made a choice to let that teacher program your beliefs: "I am shy." And your subconscious has been supporting that label on yourself ever since junior high.

If you want to re-program your beliefs to be consistent with your goals and dreams, remember that you are ultimately in charge of your beliefs. Take inventory — keep the winning beliefs, continually add supporting beliefs, and delete your false, self-limiting beliefs!

Ask Yourself Great Questions

We should not only master questions, but also act upon them, and act definitely.
—Woodrow T. Wilson, Twenty-eighth president of the United States

*I*F YOU CONSCIOUSLY IMPROVE the quality of your questions, you will drastically improve the quality of your thoughts.

Our thoughts are manufactured by the constant questions we ask ourselves. Again, like most of the principles in this book, most people are allowing this process to happen without knowing it.

For example, if you feel depressed, you may ask yourself, "Why am I always so depressed these days?" It sounds like an innocent enough question — you are only trying to find an answer, right?

When you ask any question, it is your mind's job to search its "database" and find an answer that reinforces the question — and that is exactly what happens. So if you ask a self-defeating question like, "Why am I always depressed?" you may get an answer like, "You are always depressed because life is cruel and unfair." This kind of answer will create even more depression.

31

If you replace the self-defeating question with an empowering question like, "What can I do, today, to start to feel like myself — the enthusiastic, happy, and motivated person who gets the most out of life?" you will get a far better answer. In this case you will get a solution!

8

Self-Worth

Your worth consists in what you are ... not in what you have.
—Thomas Edison, American inventor

WHAT ARE YOU WORTH? Many people answer this question with a dollar figure.

How much money you have is important — we obviously need money to buy food, clothes, and shelter. How much stuff you have (cars, boats, self-cleaning microwaves, gadgets, and other toys) is less important. What people say about you is even less important.

Your real self-worth has nothing to do with financial wealth, material possessions, acknowledgements, degrees, contacts, employee-of-the-month awards, or any outside recognition. Why? Because these things won't make you happy! How else can we explain the suicides and drug addictions of so many famous entertainers, business tycoons, and star athletes who "had it all"? These people had money, accolades, praise, admiration, and fame, but they were miserable.

Perhaps they didn't realize that self-worth can only come from within. Your self-worth can be measured every time you look in the mirror. Do you like what you see when you greet yourself each morning? How happy are you to be you?

Self-worth is developed by being true to your higher self, being honest with yourself and with everyone in your life, serving a cause that's outside your own self interest, honoring your values, practicing integrity — and by the amount of love that you give.

Mother Teresa didn't have much money but she was extremely wealthy — she never compromised her integrity.

So if you want to increase your self-worth, start with the goal of developing a character that is rich with values. If you really want to "have it all," then find a cause that is bigger than yourself and give one hundred per cent of yourself to it.

And if you're going to be concerned about anyone's approval — make sure the person in the mirror is first in line!

Be Yourself

**All good things
which exist are
fruits of originality.**
—John Stuart Mill,
British philosopher

N O ONE ELSE on this whole planet has the same DNA or fingerprint as you do.

No one else has the exact same tastes, opinions, and personality as you do.

We all have some similarities with everyone else — we all want to be loved, valued, accepted, and needed (although many people are too stubborn to admit this universal truth). But no one else will ever see the world exactly the same way you do.

When you think about that for a minute, it is pretty amazing. It's kind of ironic that there is so much pressure on you to fit into a specific mold. Advertisers capitalize on our desire to be accepted by seductively selling us on the benefits of being a Marlboro Man, eating the Breakfast of Champions, and being part of the Pepsi Generation.

Instead of being identified by who we are, what we believe in, and what we value, we have been conditioned to identify ourselves with the products and services we consume.

Why would someone pay $10,000 for a watch? They may say they bought the watch for the "state of the art" engineering, the hundred-year tradition of the watch company, and the re-sale value. That all sounds pretty good but — *$10,000?* The fact is, they were sold on the illusion that having a nice watch will make them appear successful, make them accepted, and have value.

Have you ever met someone who only wore a certain brand of clothes? These people are walking advertisements; no longer individuals, they are statements.

The sooner you realize that all image is an illusion, the sooner you'll realize that the only commercial worth listening to is the one that sells you on how wonderful you are; the commercial that lists all your selling features; the commercial that raves about how wonderful it is to be you!

Fall in Love with Yourself

You will always have to live with yourself, and it is to your best interest to see that you have good company — a clean, pure, straight, honest, upright, generous, magnanimous companion.
—Orison Swett Marden, American author and founder of *Success* magazine

*L*OVE IS THE MOST PRECIOUS things on earth. Without love, life doesn't have much meaning.

Some people believe that it is arrogant to love yourself. One universal truth that applies to love is this: "You can't give away what you don't have." It is impossible to love anyone else if you don't love yourself first.

The majority of people in the world are not in love with themselves. We're conditioned from an early age to believe that we are somehow flawed. Our consumer-driven society has become preoccupied with the products and services that seductively promise to cover up these flaws. If you're presently not in love with yourself you need to do one thing: accept yourself as is.

Once you accept yourself, you can convey love to yourself in a number of ways; exercising, eating nutritious foods, and reading inspirational material are three great starters.

When you look in the mirror, take a few seconds to really appreciate who you are now and who you are becoming. Tell yourself something nice about how you look or feel.

Although this exercise may seem trite, don't underestimate the power of positive self-talk. Remember that you become your thoughts and when your thoughts are loving you will get the most out of life!

11

Write Your Own Commercial

*D*URING THE COURSE of an average day, we are inundated with thousands of commercials for virtually every product we could ever use and many more we will never use. Although you may not be consciously aware of it, your own self-commercial is running all the time.

Have you ever had thoughts like: "I'm always late," or "I'm too fat," or "I'm not very attractive"? As we've seen, these thoughts are reinforced in your subconscious, and then developed into a belief system that in turn creates your reality. If you believe you're insecure, it's because you have built a successful advertising campaign selling yourself the image of an insecure you.

Again, most of us do this unconsciously. All these mini-commercials can rob you of your self-confidence and prevent you from getting the most out of life. Understanding this mind technology and harnessing it successfully will give you a leg up on your quest to live in the realm of your higher self!

Write your own commercial. Who else stands to benefit from being sold on yourself more than you do? What are your main "selling" features? Take a few moments and write, in a hardcover blank journal, all the wonderful strengths and qualities that make it so exciting to be you. Get excited about this exercise — this is your life!

After you are finished, make a recording of yourself reading (with unbridled enthusiasm) your self-commercial. For extra effect, I suggest you play some kind of inspirational music in the background as you read your self-commercial. (The theme to *Rocky*, "Gonna Fly Now," works for me!)

You may even want to create other self-commercials for your career, your relationships, and your exercise program.

Remember, people who live extraordinary lives are willing to do what ordinary people are not. Don't be ordinary! Do this exercise!

12

Free Your Past

*T*O CREATE A POWERFUL FUTURE for your life, you must learn to release your past.

Two of the most common stumbling blocks to getting the most out of life are recurring negative thought patterns and identifying yourself with events of the past.

Most people are not even aware of how or why they see the world the way they do; they're too caught up in all the mini-urgencies of the day. Often, negative events that have happened five, ten, or even twenty years ago are unconsciously framing our perception of who we are today. For example, if you were verbally or physically abused, grew up in a home with an alcoholic parent, or perhaps were terribly shy as a child, you may be living your life today through the lens of these debilitating memories without realizing it.

However, it is time to realize that the person you are today and the person you will become tomorrow are ultimately decided by the choices you make, the beliefs you adopt, and the story that you continue to write about your life. Once you know this, your life begins to have a whole new sense of freedom and power.

The first day you realize that your story can be created in the here and now will be the last day that your past will have any significant impact on your life. It is only then that you will realize that your past is like the wake of a boat — behind you!

13

Face Your Fears

Only your mind can produce fear.
—Dr. Helen Schucman, author of *A Course in Miracles*

*I*T'S NORMAL TO HAVE FEARS. Many of our fears are healthy, like the fear of jumping out of moving cars, getting too close to wild animals, and playing with fire. These fears keep you alive.

But fear of failure, poverty, sickness, rejection, and criticism are some of the most common types of fear. These fears can prevent you from getting the most out of life.

In order to master your fears, you need to understand why you have them. Our society teaches us to fear the "unknown." From a very young age we are taught to avoid risk, uncertainty, and anything else that could be considered "unknown." Many of us have been conditioned (by well-meaning parents) to imagine the worst-case scenario if we take a certain risk.

And since tomorrow is "unknown," we're taught to fear it too. But the rest of your life is nothing but a limited number of tomorrows. To fear tomorrow is to fear life!

You will only be able to embrace the "unknown" when you can understand and appreciate its gift. The unknown is what makes life an adventure. Tomorrow is somewhat of a mystery; we don't know exactly what is going to happen. But when you realize that this "not knowing" is what keeps life interesting, exciting, and fresh, you will begin to appreciate its value. When this happens, fear loses its grip on you. It may never go away completely, but it won't incapacitate you any longer.

14

Understand Suffering

*A*s long as there has been human life, there has been suffering. Suffering is part of life, just as the afternoon is part of the day. The question shouldn't be "How can I avoid suffering?" because you won't. The question should be, "What can I learn from suffering?"

I still ask why the events of September 11 happened, why diseases like AIDS exist, and how a happy little two-year-old can die of cancer.

Is it possible that these terrible things happen to teach us something so we can evolve as a people? Could some of this suffering be happening to teach us compassion? To remind us that we are not separate from everyone else — that each one of us is a cell in a body called humanity? Could suffering be moving us closer to understanding, communicating, and connecting with our source?

I do believe everything happens for a reason. Most of the suffering that you will experience, such as the death of a loved

We are threatened with suffering from three directions: from our own body, which is doomed to decay and dissolution and which cannot even do without pain and anxiety as warning signals; from the external world, which may rage against us with overwhelming and merciless forces of destruction; and finally from our relations to other men. The suffering which comes from the last source is perhaps more painful than any other.
—Sigmund Freud, Founder of psychoanalysis

one, will remind you to live — to really live.

Other forms of suffering like sickness, poverty, and loneliness all have lessons as well. If we never experience sickness, we won't fully appreciate health; if we never experience failure, we can't enjoy success, and if we never experience anxiety we can never fully appreciate peace of mind.

15

Commit to Self-Evolution

*I*N EVERY MOMENT of every day, life offers nuggets of wisdom for all those who are aware.

Most people are too blinded by their own self-indulged plights to see the wisdom that is available to all who possess an open mind.

Think how exciting life must be for those who are committed to making the most of every day, to the point that they see every situation as an opportunity for their soul to grow and their potential to expand!

When you release your prejudices, criticism, limiting beliefs, and fear of your own potential, you will start to learn the lessons of the day.

And when you do, each morning you will awaken to a higher self. Each day, your knowledge of the ways of the world will grow and as it does you will experience a sense of well-being that can only be described with one word: *heavenly.*

Section 2
The Proper Tools

(16)

Get Enough Sleep

*T*ODAY IT SEEMS that we're busier than ever.

The advances in technology that were supposed to give us more time seem instead to *take* more of our time. Emails, faxes, voicemail, cellphones, and instant messages are all competing for your attention. It seems like you need 48 hours in a day to meet all the demands on your time.

As a result of these increased demands, far too many people are trying to do more on less sleep. Lack of sleep can make you cranky, short-tempered, and irritable.

Medical research has proven that without a minimum of six hours' sleep you lose focus, have more difficulty concentrating, and experience less joy.

You need sleep to be energized; even enthusiasm fizzles out without a well-rested body. Ultimately, without enough sleep you won't have enough energy to pursue your goals.

Remember, if you want to give a hundred per cent in your life you have to perform at a hundred per cent of your potential. Think of sleep as an opportunity to recharge your batteries.

Eat Healthy Foods

WE SEEM TO BE LIVING in a time when we're prioritizing speed and convenience ahead of quality and nutrition when it comes to deciding how and when to eat.

The large restaurant chains have introduced somewhat healthier menus in the past few years to hold on to their ever-decreasing share of the baby boomer market. They'd better; over 70 million baby boomers are entering a stage of life where they have to watch everything they eat. Obesity, high blood pressure, hardening of the arteries, and diabetes are common topics of conversation among them. Decades of french fries, hamburgers, and milkshakes are finally catching up.

What's the point of sacrificing nutrition today, while you're working, to spend all your time at the doctor's office when you retire? Healthy eating takes more of an effort but it's worth it. You'll live longer, you'll feel better, and you'll have more energy.

Measure your health by your sympathy with morning and spring. If there is no response in you to the awakening of nature — if the prospect of an early morning walk does not banish sleep — if the warble of the first bluebird does not thrill you — know that the morning and spring of your life are past. Thus you may feel your pulse.

—Henry David Thoreau, American essayist, poet and naturalist

(18)

Exercise Regularly

WHEN WE EXERCISE, our bodies release endorphins — the body's feel-good medicine.

These "natural drugs" are the best on the market: they're free, they give you a wonderful it's-great-to-be-alive feeling, and they're good for you.

People who exercise on a regular basis have a better outlook on life, have more energy, are more productive, and live longer. You'll notice that you will react better to stress and be less anxious once you adopt an exercise routine.

You don't have to become an Arnold Schwarzenegger, run the Boston Marathon, or even join a gym. You may discover that having a good walk before work is enough to get results.

Honor Your Values

It's not hard to make decisions when you know what your values are.

—Roy Disney, American film producer, Walt Disney's nephew

*A*LL TOO OFTEN IN LIFE, we discover that the big things we pursued turned out to be the little things and the little things turned out to be the big things.

Have you ever felt like you're just spinning your wheels? This happens when your priorities are not aligned with your values.

The best way to differentiate the little things from the big things is to clarify your values. What do you value most in life?

Make a list of your top 10 values. Your values may include personal growth, social contribution, family, wisdom, prosperity, freedom, adventure, spirituality, and love. Now prioritize them, listing the four most important. Next, pick your top two values.

This exercise will tell you where you should be spending the majority of your time; it will also help you define your main purpose in life.

Define
Your Purpose

I BELIEVE EVERYONE has one unique talent to offer the world. Unfortunately, most people have their unique talent buried under a pile of to-do lists that have nothing to do with their true calling. They are too busy being busy to take the time to figure out what they are here to do.

People who live with purpose have a spring in their step, fire in their belly, and passion in their eyes, telling the world they're alive in the true sense of the word. Until we can become one with our purpose, we will continue to have a feeling in our gut that we're missing something — no matter how much stuff we accumulate.

We all have a song to sing; even if we are not singing it at the moment, our heart will periodically give us clues about what that song is.

Make a list of all your skills, qualities, and values. Write down what you're absolutely passionate about. Include everything that motivates and inspires you. This will point you in the right direction.

To put away aimlessness and weakness, and to begin to think with purpose, is to enter the ranks of those strong ones who only recognize failure as one of the pathways to attainment, who make all conditions serve them, and who think strongly, attempt fearlessly, and accomplish masterfully.

—James Allen, American essayist

Write Down Your Goals

Man is a goal-seeking animal. His life only has meaning if he is reaching out and striving for his goals.

—Aristotle, Greek philosopher

M OST PEOPLE live in a world of "someday." How many times have you heard someone say: "Someday I'm going to have money," or "Someday I'm going to have my own business," or "Someday I'm going to be in a great relationship"?

When you live in a world of "someday," the weeks turn into months, the months turn into years, and before you know it you're at the end of your life. Unfortunately, this is how most people live. It's as if they're waiting for their ship to come in. Isn't this why the lottery organizations do so well?

The best way to make someday *today* is to write down what you want out of life — write down your goals. It's not enough to say, "I already know what I want; I don't need to write anything down."

We expect our government leaders to have goals for our country and the companies we invest in to have long-term goals for their organizations, yet we often fail to see the need to write goals for our own lives. Does that make sense? Usually people don't write down their goals because of low self-esteem, unconsciously thinking: "Oh, what's the point, I'm not going to accomplish any of these."

But that's the pattern we're here to break. Write down goals for all of the most important areas of your life: family, career, finances, personal growth, spirituality, and health. Have short-, medium- and long-term goals and review your progress on a regular basis.

The very act of writing down your goals will take you one step closer to getting the most out of life!

Prioritize

The more
priorities, the
fewer urgencies.
—Gino Ciaveralla,
Wealth management
guru

O NCE YOU HAVE written down your goals in all of the important areas of your life (family, career, health, finance, personal growth, and spirituality), you may feel a bit overwhelmed, especially if you've tackled your short-, medium- and long-term goals. You may wonder how you are ever going to accomplish all these goals. The answer, in a word, is: *prioritizing*.

Start with one set of goals — let's say, the annual ones. Prioritize them into three groups according to their significance to you. Your most important goals could be called the "A" goals (these are *must*-dos). Next come your "B" goals (*should*-dos) and finally, your "C" goals (*could*-dos).

Then you prioritize within each group. Go back to each category and number each goal in the "A" category according to its importance, then do this for your "B" and "C" goals as well.

This system is as basic as it gets — and it works. The next step is to use some kind of time-organizer to block off time for each goal. Once this task is finished, you're well on your way to accomplishing anything you set your mind to.

Have Faith

You can do very
little with faith,
but you can do
nothing without it.
—Samuel Butler,
British writer

*F*AITH IS THE SONG the songbird sings each morning before the dawn.

To have faith is to believe in what you do not see. Sooner or later, with faith, you will see what you believe. The Bible tells us, "If ye have faith as a grain of mustard-seed, ye shall say unto this mountain, remove hence to yonder place; and it shall remove." Without this intangible element, goals will remain little more than good intentions.

To turn your dreams into reality you need to harness faith to the chariot of your imagination. Visualize the results you want to create financially, physically, and spiritually, in your relationships, your career, and any other area of your life.

Once you have a set of clearly defined goals and a strategy to accomplish them, faith will attract (through the power of the subconscious) everything else that you will ever need, including opportunities and resources. This is the "law of attraction." See chapter 36 for more on this important principle.

(24)

Take Action

It takes as much energy to wish as it does to plan.
—Eleanor Roosevelt, American First Lady and humanitarian

PEOPLE OFTEN GET STUCK after they write down their goals, as if they think their goals are somehow going to manifest themselves on their own. It just doesn't work that way. After you have defined your goals clearly, you will need to take massive action.

Your goals will only be accomplished by implementing a strategy that is broken down into a series of action steps. Every step required to accomplish each goal should have a due date. This isn't rocket science — it just takes a little patience and a whole lot of planning. Start today.

Look at the goals you've written for the next year. Start off with one category, say "Finance," and write the action steps with due dates to make every single goal happen.

When you actually sit down and write your strategy, you'll start to feel overwhelmingly more optimistic about your future because you're not leaving it up to chance.

25

Master Your Time

A man who dares to waste one hour of his life has not discovered the value of life.
—Charles Darwin, British naturalist

*T*IME IS A COMMODITY that you have less and less of every day.

The U.S. News and World Report has stated that we will spend up to five years of our lives standing in line. Other news organizations have reported that we will spend between seven and ten years of our lives watching television.

Of course, you have total control over how much time you spend in front of a television set, but you can't always control how long you'll spend waiting in line, whether in traffic, at government agencies, or in waiting rooms.

One way to take control of potential time-wasters is to carry something to read. Be prepared to wait. I actually look forward to waiting now, so I can catch up on my reading.

Invest in a pocket computer, or personal digital assistant (PDA). With your PDA you can review your goals, revise your strategies, update your to-do list, write a memo, or update your address file.

If you do a lot of driving, always keep personal development audio recordings in your car. In no time you'll be referring to your car as your "library on wheels!"

(26)

Don't Be a
Couch Potato

ACCORDING TO recent studies, teenagers today spend 33 to 35 hours a week watching television.

The average 14-year-old male will have witnessed more than 12,000 television murders. The scary thing about that statistic is that your subconscious mind does not know the difference between fantasy and reality when it is incorporating what you see and hear into the deepest parts of your mind.

Adults aren't much better. Even after working 40 or 50 hours per week, we're still spending 14 to 16 hours a week watching television.

Vegetating in front of a television will suck the life right out of you if you're watching programs that are in direct conflict with the objectives of your higher self. We've become a nation of spectators. Life doesn't reward spectators. You've heard the saying, "Life is not a spectator sport."

So how do you wean yourself off television? Take inventory of the programs you watch from Monday to Sunday. Beside each television show write down a minimum of three things that you could be doing that would create more excitement, joy, and fun in your life. What activities do you really enjoy but haven't had the time to do? Could you be replacing some television time with exercise or family time? Maybe there's a great book you've been meaning to read.

After doing this exercise, you may find an additional 10 hours a week to get the most out of life!

Don't Procrastinate

Things may come to those who wait, but only the things left by those who hustle.
—Abraham Lincoln, Sixteenth president of the United States

*T*HE GREAT Roman emperor Marcus Aurelius said, "Think of your many years of procrastination; how the gods have repeatedly granted you further periods of grace, of which you have taken no advantage.

"It is time now to realize the nature of the universe to which you belong, and of that controlling Power whose offspring you are, and to understand that your time has a limit set to it. Use it, then, to advance your enlightenment; or it will be gone, and never in your power again."

If you live to be 80 years old, you will have lived a mere 29,200 days on this wonderful planet. If you're 40 right now you've already lived 14,600 days.

We must remember that each day of our life is an amazing gift. Each day, we're given the gift of 86,400 seconds to get the most out of life. What if we paid a dollar per second? Would that create a sense of urgency to get our money's worth out of this day?

Unfortunately, most people squander their time until an illness, setback, or disaster strikes. We are all guilty, to various degrees, of wasting time in some way or other. We really do act as if we're going to live forever.

The sure-fire way to end procrastination is to assign deadlines to all your goals, define your purpose in life, and take ongoing, tenacious action. Live your life with a healthy sense of urgency to accomplish your goals, live up to your full potential, and leave a legacy.

Do this and you'll have no time to procrastinate!

(28)

Be Persistent

I am a slow walker, but I never walk backwards.

—Abraham Lincoln, Sixteenth president of the United States

SUCCESSFUL PEOPLE see setbacks as opportunities to learn and grow, often finding clues in each failure or crisis that will ultimately lead to success.

The Chinese character for "crisis" is the same as the one for "opportunity."

Thomas Edison, inventor of the incandescent light bulb, had only three months of formal education. That's often considered reason enough to be a quitter. Did you know that he apparently failed, while trying to invent the incandescent light bulb, several thousand times?

If anyone had a reason to give up, it was him. Mr. Edison wasn't a quitter; in fact, he had a sign in his office that read, "There is a better way — find it." A young journalist asked Mr. Edison how he finally invented the incandescent light bulb after failing so many times. His response was, "I had to succeed … I finally ran out of ways that wouldn't work."

What could you achieve with an attitude like Mr. Edison's? Abraham Lincoln failed in business and he failed in politics. He failed at pretty much everything he tried; he even had a nervous breakdown, before becoming the sixteenth president of the United States.

The major difference between the people who achieve success in life and those who do not is their perception of failure. When you decide to commit to living your life to your fullest potential (as few people do), when you can see in your mind's eye the outcome you want in your life, you will be persistent.

And when you begin to find opportunity in every crisis, you'll be well on your way to getting the most out of life.

(29)

Clean House

*G*ETTING THE MOST OUT OF LIFE requires periodic house cleaning.

Write a list of the habits you have right now that are working in your life, habits that allow you to be more productive, that give you more peace of mind, and that guide you in the right direction on your quest to live to your fullest potential.

Some of your good habits may include regular exercise, writing and reviewing your weekly, monthly, and yearly goals, meditating, writing about life's lessons in a journal, and eating nutritious foods.

Reviewing your positive habits will give you a bird's eye view of which strengths work and what still needs work. Now look at your list: what positive habits could you add to your list that would give you even better results?

Next, write a list of habits that are getting in the way, slowing you down, and adding stress to your life. Really study that list, and write down the long-term consequences of keeping these habits.

Then write down what you need to do to correct these habits. What action are you going to take *today* to replace these self-defeating habits with life-empowering habits that will inspire you to get the most out of life?

Live Simply

Our life is frittered away by detail. Simplify, simplify, simplify! I say, let your affairs be as two or three, and not a hundred or a thousand. Instead of a million count half a dozen, and keep your accounts on your thumbnail.
—Henry David Thoreau, American writer and naturalist

*H*AVE YOU EVER considered how many advertisements you watch each week?

If there is one common theme to the flow of endless commercials and ads, it's that we need more stuff. We're taught that the stuff we have isn't as good as the stuff that we should buy today.

It's tempting to buy more stuff. I always ask myself when I'm being hypnotized by an ad, "Do I really need this?" The answer is "no" 99.9 per cent of the time.

Simplicity is being able to find anything you need any time you need it. Living simply means taking inventory of your life.

Stop and think for a minute about the habits you may have developed that contribute to your clutter. Do you buy stuff you don't really need just because it's on sale?

What other habits do you have that contribute to your clutter? Get rid of them. The long-term impact of having too much stuff is a cluttered life. Practice simplicity — you'll have much more peace of mind.

Develop Self-Discipline

W HEN YOU PRACTICE self-discipline on a regular basis, your willpower will begin to take on a life of its own. Lack of willpower may prevent you from creating the consistency needed to attain your goals.

It takes self-discipline to actually do all the steps necessary to reach each goal. With so many choices about how to spend our time, it becomes all too easy to get off track. Most people do.

It's not enough to have good intentions; we all have good intentions. We need good *habits*. To have good habits, we need to be motivated. Your challenge will be to stay motivated enough to resist all the temptations that beg for your time.

In your mind's eye, you need to visualize how you will feel as you accomplish each goal. See yourself wearing that size-eight bathing suit. Visualize how much more energy you will have with 30 fewer pounds on your body.

Only when you have "emotionalized" your desired goals in this way will there be any hope for acquiring self-discipline.

Section 3

The Search for the Higher Self

32

Seek Wisdom

*E*VERY NOW AND THEN I meet people who have lukewarm attitudes about personal development. They might say: "Oh, I've read those kinds of books already," meaning they have finished discovering, growing, and learning.

Did you know that if you committed 12 hours a day for the rest of your life to learning from the wisdom of people like Confucius, Helen Keller, and Marcus Aurelius, you would just be scratching the surface?

Wisdom is available for the taking, not just from the books you read but in everyday experiences. You can even find wisdom while standing in line at your bank. If you could hear people's thoughts while waiting in line, you might hear comments like: "How come every time I come here I have to wait?" or "This is ridiculous, why are they so slow?!"

Instead, you could choose to learn from the expression on the 90-year-old's face right in front of you. Over the years, maybe she has learned to recognize life's beauty everywhere. Maybe she isn't complaining about how slowly the line is moving. No, she is soaking up the smiles of the three-year-old in front of her. She is connecting with the world.

Being wise means knowing that every moment of life is your whole life; it means being aware that you can choose the outcome, emotion, and reaction in every situation. It means knowing the cost of being reactive and the value of being proactive.

Our potential and the universe have a common trait: both are infinite. In life, you have a world of opportunities to grow, learn, and stretch. Sadly, most people seldom venture outside their spiritual front door.

Look at your life as you would an ongoing experiment whose goal is to continuously expand your potential, consciousness, and wisdom. If you consciously seek wisdom, before long you'll actually feel its ever-increasing presence, its calming effect, and its certainty in you at all times.

Be Aware

B E AWARE of your thoughts, actions, and speech. Learn to see the long-term consequences of everything you do.

Most of society today functions in a semi-comatose-like state. We unconsciously follow a pattern of daily routines — so much so that for most people each day looks pretty much like the one before. Not thinking beyond the minimum daily requirements has become the norm!

The way most people live their life reminds me of an experiment conducted by the great French naturalist, John Henry Fabre, on processionary caterpillars. These creatures robotically follow each other in procession, one after the other. Fabre placed some of these caterpillars in a circle, so that the lead caterpillar actually touched the last one, to make a complete circle. In the center of the circle Fabre placed pine needles, food for these caterpillars. They walked around the circle for 24 hours, then 48 hours, then 72 hours, and then a week — without taking a break for rest or food. Finally, they dropped dead from starvation and exhaustion.

Like these caterpillars, most people today mistake activity for accomplishment and end up exhausted and disappointed.

Like anything worthwhile, learning to be aware takes practice and discipline. Take time to reflect daily, whether it's writing in a journal, going for a walk, or meditating; you'll only get the most out of life when you're aware of the awesome potential that lies within you, in your environment, and in every moment. Only then will you see that you're not a caterpillar — you're a butterfly!

(34)

Take Inventory of Your Beliefs

*A*S WE HAVE SEEN over and over in this book, every action, emotion, and thought is influenced by our dominating beliefs. So it's important to understand which beliefs are creating the results you want and which beliefs are sabotaging your life.

When you take the time to identify your limiting beliefs you will be in a better position to remove any self-imposed limitations that have been preventing you from designing your life.

Take out your journal or a blank piece of paper. On the right side of the page, list all your beliefs about yourself and the world that fuel your spirit to get the most out of life. A positive belief about you may be, "If I give a hundred per cent in life I will be successful," or "If I exercise on a regular basis I will feel better and be healthier."

On the left side of the page, list all the negative beliefs you have of yourself and the world that rob you of opportunity.

A negative belief is any belief that prevents you from being your best — for example, "I can't get ahead since I only have a high school education and all the good jobs go to university graduates." (I'll remind you that Thomas Edison, inventor of the incandescent light bulb, only had three months of formal education.)

Once you've identified the negative beliefs, take a few minutes to study them. Keep the ones you want and retire the rest. Remember, all negative beliefs about your own potential are figments of your imagination!

Retire any limiting beliefs and replace them with supportive, powerful, and inspiring beliefs.

Believe in Miracles

*I*N THE LAST HUNDRED YEARS, we have invented technologies such as cell phones, microwave ovens, and satellite television. We've harnessed radio waves, split atoms, and even walked on the moon. Two hundred years ago, if you told anyone about these kinds of future advances in civilization you would have been locked up! One word would have been used to describe these types of impossibilities: *miracles.*

Albert Einstein and Thomas Edison believed in miracles — what else would have kept Mr. Edison going after failing to invent the incandescent light bulb several thousand times? Mr. Einstein lived by the saying, "There are only two ways to look at your life. One is as though nothing is a miracle. The other is as though everything is a miracle." It's that easy and yet it's also that difficult.

In the year 2200, we will have a cure for cancer and world peace — yes, even in the Middle East. AIDS will have been eradicated and world hunger will not exist. (Teenagers, however, will still be annoying.)

These advances will happen all because someone believed in miracles. As always, there will be more non-believers than believers, and as always miracles will continue to happen. And as always, those who truly believe that anything is possible will continue to get the most out of life.

What kind of miracles do you need to happen in your life? Do you need more money, a better career, or a relationship makeover, or do you just need to lose a few pounds? What has the cost been so far of *not* believing in miracles? Or, look at it another way: What have you *gained* by not believing in them?

Don't just think about these questions and then move on to the next page — take out your journal and start writing!

(36)

Meditate

In deep meditation the flow of concentration is continuous like the flow of oil.

—Patanjali, Author of *How to Know God* and the creator of yoga

*O*NE OF THE GREATEST WAYS to relax and find peace of mind and clarity is through meditation. Meditation has been practiced for more than two thousand years.

There are many benefits to giving yourself 20 to 30 minutes each day of silence, reflection, and connection to your higher self. Meditation will help you find an inner wisdom, not only to guide you through life, but also to create opportunities to manifest your desires.

Though there are many different types of meditation, its basic principle is to focus your mind on a thought or an object. I suggest you read a few books on the topic or take a course to learn more. There are two kinds of mediation that I practice: transcendental and japa.

In transcendental meditation, you repeat a phrase or "mantra." For example, you may repeat a phrase like "Om Mani Padme Hum." This Sanskrit mantra is one of the most widely used in the world today, and means "God." The purpose of this type of meditation is to quiet the mind, find peace, and connect with your source.

In japa meditation, the goal is to focus on what you want to create in your life. When I practice japa I focus on the goals I want to accomplish. In my mind's eye, I see myself successfully accomplishing my goals. Japa meditation will harness the law of attraction to bring into physical form that which is created in the mind's eye.

The law of attraction is practiced (in most cases unconsciously) by everyone on the planet, but understood by few. Its basic premise is that every thought you have produces an energy, and this energy attracts other similar energies. Think about it. Have you ever needed a certain amount of money in a limited time period and then, out of nowhere, the money finds you through an "opportunity?"

These sorts of circumstances are not merely coincidences. This is a universal power that can create either abundance or chaos, so be careful what you focus your thoughts on.

Meditation is one of the best ways to learn to master this life-altering tool. If practiced regularly, with pure intention, this exercise will take you to unimaginable heights.

Practice Visualization

*Y*OUR GOALS will become substantially easier to attain if you harness the magic of visualization technology.

Don't worry, you don't need to buy software or take a computer course; you were born with this technology in your head.

Look at any of the most successful people in business, athletics, or the arts — one common thread between these super-triumphant people is their mastery of visualization techniques.

They often use visualization unconsciously to create momentum on their way to achieving their goals. Others make a daily practice of visualizing the kind of person they want to become, the goals they want to achieve, and the life they want to design.

You may have heard the story of an American prisoner of war, Major James Nesmeth, who was in jail in North Vietnam for seven years. During the entire time, Major Nesmeth was held in solitary

> My method is different. I do not rush into actual work. When I get a new idea, I start at once building it up in my imagination, and make improvements and operate the device in my mind. When I have gone so far as to embody everything in my invention, every possible improvement I can think of, and when I see no fault anywhere, I put into concrete form the final product of my brain.
>
> —Nikola Tesla, Croatian-American physicist and inventor

confinement, in a cage that was approximately four-and-a-half feet high and five feet long (1.4 meters by 1.5 meters). His captors did not allow him any physical activity. Major Nesmeth soon realized he had to find some way to take his mind off the terrible conditions he was in. Since he was a golfer, he chose to imagine playing golf. Every day, he imagined playing a perfect game of golf at his favorite country club. He never missed a shot. The visualization technique worked so well that when he was freed and finally got to play a real game of golf he took 20 strokes off his game to shoot a 74!

Remember, your subconscious does not know the difference between reality and fantasy. When you spend time visualizing yourself achieving your goals, you're conditioning yourself mentally and spiritually to create your desired outcome. Each time you visualize yourself accomplishing your goals, you are also creating positive emotions that will be stored in the subconscious mind. These memories will actually create momentum when you are in a "real life" situation. Your body and mind will respond as they have been conditioned to respond in your mind's eye.

Make visualization a daily part of your success rituals and see for yourself how much easier it becomes to get the most out of life.

Pay Attention to the Seasons of Life

Live in each season as it passes; breathe the air, drink the drink, taste the fruit, and resign yourself to the influences of each. Let them be your only diet and drink botanical medicines.
—Henry David Thoreau, American essayist

*H*AVE YOU EVER wondered why we have a spring, summer, fall, and winter season? Could this be God's loving way of reminding us that *we* have seasons too?

In the spring, notice the new life in the trees and flowers as they blossom. Witness the hope, potential, and excitement that spring represents. Summer is to be enjoyed without a care in the world — no reminders, just lots of long summer days to celebrate life.

As the leaves change color in the fall you're reminded how beautiful life is. And no sooner do the red, orange, and yellow colors of autumn orchestrate their finest hour do you begin to notice the nights get a little colder. Winter's breath is on your skin to remind you that soon life will be no more. As the ground turns cold and nature retreats into winter, you're reminded that death is coming, so live with all your might.

How fortunate we are to have these gentle reminders to enjoy the moments

and live with a healthy sense of urgency!
God is so kind: she gives us, on average,
75 to 85 yearly reminders to pay attention
to life and live to our fullest potential.

Have *you* been paying attention to the
seasons?

(39)

Celebrate Your Death

WHAT? YES, you read that correctly. I know it sounds strange, but let me explain. Have you ever considered why so many people are afraid of death? Well, there are the obvious reasons: not knowing what it will feel like to die, or how, or when. There's the fear of not knowing exactly what will happen next and where you will go. We live in an information age where it stresses us out not to know something, especially something that lurks deep in our thoughts. As discussed in "Face Your Fears" (chapter 13), we're taught to fear anything we don't know, and death is to many the mother of unknowns.

We fear death, but we fear something else even more, and that is the failure to live life to its fullest potential.

We all have an intuitive understanding that we are awesome, powerful, and somehow connected to a source of unlimited strength, love, and unison. We know that there is a place within us that is one with everything. Meditation is one way to get to that place. Another is to celebrate your death each day.

Each morning, when you awaken, find a quiet place and visualize your death as a celebration! When you visualize your life, start with your lifeless body, then rewind in your mind's eye and see yourself at different stages of your life. Spend your time on the parts that haven't happened yet. See yourself living a life that has harnessed its source. See yourself living fully, happily, and peacefully. See yourself accomplishing your heart's desires!

Make this exercise a part of your daily ritual and prepare for the magic to unfold. Prepare to become one with your dreams!

(40)

Write Your Own Eulogy

WHETHER YOU LIKE IT OR NOT, you are going to die.

We don't like to think about dying. This is a big mistake, because the more we think about dying, the more we realize how precious life is and how it must be lived to the fullest.

When you take the time to write your eulogy, you are communicating how you would like to be remembered. You are also declaring how you would like to live your life. Write your eulogy!

Write down five character traits that you would like to describe the kind of person you were. After you write down these five character traits, look at them. Do you embody these traits now? No? Then you have some work to do!

What five accomplishments do you want to be remembered for? What five contributions to the world do you want to be remembered for? Remember, your contributions don't have to be as grand as finding a cure for cancer or creating peace in the Middle East — although these miracles will happen too. Your contributions could be making a difference in the life of a child, making your neighborhood a friendlier place to live in, or simply the acts of kindness you offer to every soul you ever meet.

What five outrageously exciting and adventurous things did you do in your life?

The benefit of completing this exercise is life altering. You will have defined what the rest of your life will be about. You will also have built a very powerful tool to remind yourself of how the rest of your life is to be lived. This tool will be of the most use when you periodically get off course, which we all do from time to time. Now go out and make it happen!

And when people stop you in the street and say, "What are you so excited about?" You can say: "I'm creating my eulogy." Yes, you will get some strange looks.

(41)

Listen to Music

NOTHING CARESSES THE SOUL the way music does.

How many times have you heard an old song on the radio and found yourself immediately whisked away to another time and place? You can almost touch the people and places that were in your life at that particular time.

When I hear the song *We're Here for a Good Time* by a Canadian band called Trooper, I'm immediately brought back to Amherst, Nova Scotia. I was 12 years old and injured from racing my motorcycle in my first (and last) motocross race. Five minutes into the race I was laid out on the ground with six people around me. As I screamed in pain, the only thing I remember is the music — *We're Here for a Good Time* — and someone around me singing along. Now, every time I hear that song a warm, soothing feeling of nostalgia rushes over me.

Music can put you in a good mood, ignite your soul, or move you to tears.

When you're stressed out, music can soothe your soul and send you into a profound state of relaxation. When you're exercising, the right music can give you the inspirational boost you need to go the extra mile.

People try to explain why and how music affects us the way it does — you can even get a degree in music psychology. I can't say for sure why music affects us the way it does; all I know is that music is food for the soul and is essential for getting the most out of life!

(42)

Take a Bath

When I look back on all the worries I remember the story of the old man who said on his deathbed that he had a lot of trouble in his life, most of which never happened.
—Winston Churchill, former British prime minister

T HE WORLD SEEMS TO BE getting faster every day. It seems like we barely have time to smile at one another, never mind connect. We rush from one meeting to the next, from work to home, and from home to work.

Sometimes you just need to take a mental vacation, and one of the best ways to take a timeout from all the day-to-day pressures of life is to take a nice hot bath.

Take at least one full hour. Get your favorite soap, bubble bath, and a good book. You may want to bring in a few soaking tunes to create the proper bathing mood. Am I missing anything? Of course — your favorite beverage may hit the spot as well.

And think, while you're soaking for the next 60 minutes, about how it's the little things in life (like taking time for a bath) that are really the big things.

Most people have it backwards. Life isn't about the rat race, the stress, the corner office, or anything superficial. It's just about connection. Taking a bath gives you time to connect with yourself, to gather your thoughts, catch your breath, and realign your priorities.

(43)

Find Peace

The practice of peace and reconciliation is one of the most vital and artistic of human actions.
—Thich Nhat Hanh, Vietnamese Buddhist monk

*T*ODAY WE'RE LIVING in a time when war is not too far from our thoughts. Religious fundamentalists and their insane infatuation with war seem to be the lead stories each night as we learn of the latest attempt to rob people of life and peace of mind. It seems that every third day we learn on CNN that the CIA has uncovered yet another threat; each threat seems to be more imminent than the last.

World peace is possible, but it has to start with you. Peace is a state of mind, and like enthusiasm, it is very contagious. We create peace by putting things into perspective. Life is short. Use this ongoing threat as a wake-up call to live your life with a healthy sense of urgency to be your best. Concern yourself with what you have control over: your thoughts, beliefs, and emotions. Now would be as good a time as any to practice faith. Have faith that good will win over evil — it always does.

But most of all, create peace in your home, with your friends, with your clients, and with strangers you encounter on your way to work every day. Create peace in every nook and cranny of your life. If enough of us have internal peace, there will eventually be world peace.

(44)

Be Silent

MAKE TIME TO BE SILENT. There is a universal consciousness that has the answer to every question that has been and will be asked. One of the best ways to tap into this source of divine guidance is by being still.

Practicing silence, as well as meditation, will create a new sense of awareness, a deeper connection to your higher self, and a greater appreciation of your surroundings.

But whereas meditation is an active pursuit — to focus on a single idea or thing — silence is a deliberate emptying of the mind. All you need is 10 to 15 minutes of quality quiet time to just be.

Mother Teresa said, "We need to find God, and he cannot be found in noise and restlessness. God is the friend of silence. See how nature — trees, flowers, grass — grows in silence; see the stars, the moon and the sun, how they move in silence. We need silence to be able to touch souls."

Today, more than ever, we need to

re-connect with our source. Finding silence will give you peace of mind, inspiration, and time to reflect on the challenges of the day.

For me, the best time to be silent is first thing in the morning, just after I awaken. This is the only time of day when my mind is relatively quiet; before the concerns, worries, and challenges of the new day begin to compete for my attention. Suddenly, the answers you've been looking for will pop into your consciousness, life will seem less chaotic, and a new sense of peace and well-being will become a familiar disposition.

(45)

Enjoy Nature

Pilgrimage to the place of the wise is to find escape from the flame of separateness.

Rumi,
Persian Sufi
mystic poet

*F*IND TIME TO COMMUNE with nature. Go for a walk or a hike in the woods. Get far enough away from traffic, sirens, and noise to find serenity. Walk quietly. Take in all the sounds and sights of your natural surroundings.

In nature, your identity disappears; you are no longer the lawyer, stockbroker, teacher, or student. You are just part of nature. In nature, you are not separate from everyone and everything but part of everyone and everything. This is your true self.

I always feel a sense of renewal after a good walk in the woods. The woods have a calming effect that releases the anxieties and stresses of the day, gently nourishing the soul and getting you closer to your source. God is everywhere but is at home in nature.

Take up a new hobby that brings you back to nature. My wife Marsha and I hike and mountain bike in the warmer months and cross-country ski in the winter.

Virtually every major city in North America has public lands that are available for you to enjoy. Find out where they are and make them your new playground!

46

Invite Nature into Your Home

T HE MOST COMFORTABLE, relaxing, and peaceful homes usually have an abundance of plants and flowers.

Plants and flowers create a natural mood of tranquility, peace, and harmony. They look good too! French novelist Gerard Nerval said, "Every flower is a soul blossoming in nature."

Many hospitals have atriums to improve the recovery and morale of their patients, and with good reason. Flowers have come to symbolize love, care, and concern, three key elements needed to assist the body's healing process.

NASA scientists have even found plants to be helpful in absorbing potentially harmful household gases and generally keeping the air clean. Some plants are better than others at this: the bamboo palm, Chinese evergreen, and the peace lily are known to be among the best.

Flowers have spoken to me more than I can tell in written words. They are the hieroglyphics of angels, loved by all men for the beauty of their character, though few can decipher even fragments of their meaning.
—Lydia M. Child, American abolitionist

Write in a Journal

*O*NE OF MY GREATEST TEACHERS over the last 10 years has been my journal.

A journal records the story of your life. At the end of each day, I record the highlights and challenges found in the day's events. Often, while writing about my day, an idea will find its way onto the page, usually about a problem I'm currently working on.

The greatest value in keeping a journal is that it allows you to see your wisdom evolve. By reviewing my journal regularly, I've noticed different problems that come up over and over again. This awareness allowed me to focus my attention on the source of the problem and solve it. I'm sure that if I didn't record the lessons of the day I would still have many of the self-defeating habits that I used to have.

I also find my journal to be an ongoing source of wisdom and inspiration as I look back and read how excited I was and continue to be as I have my personal triumphs on my journey of self-discovery and growth. I can't think of a better way to reflect on your life.

Remember, you're constantly creating the story of your life — it is worth recording.

Read Inspirational Material

I HAVE READ in various behavioral science journals that 70 per cent of our thoughts are negative.

Is it any wonder? Turn on the news tonight and odds are you won't hear about all the wonderful, magnificent, and inspirational events of the day. You will see (repeatedly) a woman caught on videotape shaking her baby, an interview with a gloom-and-doom expert, and the latest crime statistics. Whether it's imminent war, stock market collapses, or politicians caught with their pants down, the news can be a depressing source of information.

Granted, it is important to know what's going on in the world. But if your dominant source of information is the evening news, it will be hard to maintain a positive outlook.

I would advise that you watch the news no more than once a week. Don't worry — if the world is going to end, someone will tell you. In the meantime, use this time to get inspired. Read up on topics that will help you cultivate the skills you need to live your life to your fullest potential. Read stories of hope, perseverance, and success. I recently read cyclist Lance Armstrong's biography and was blown away with inspiration. Actor Christopher Reeve's *Nothing is Impossible* is full of hope, inspiration, and raw courage.

You're never the same after spending a few hours with such quality company.

49

Read Biographies of Successful People

BUDDHA AND CONFUCIUS lived more than 2,500 years ago. Thomas Edison and Helen Keller lived in the last 100 years. Nelson Mandela and Loretta LaRoche are both alive at the time of this writing. All of these great men and women have something to offer you.

You'll discover, in reading biographies of successful people, there are many universal truths in life that, when applied consistently, will help you live your life at your fullest potential. In time you will begin to see the pattern of consistent actions, beliefs, and behaviors that enable one to make miracles happen, set world records, and even move mountains.

More than two thousand years ago Christ said, "Had ye but faith, ye could move mountains," and in the past two thousand years countless wise men and women of their time have moved mountains. Find out what you need to do, to be, and to know so you can move mountains too! Be a collector of wisdom.

Build a Sanctuary

The more tranquil a man becomes, the greater is his success, his influence, his power for good. Calmness of mind is one of the beautiful jewels of wisdom.
—James Allen,
Author of
As a Man Thinketh

WITH ALL THE DEMANDS on our time it's easy to feel you are losing control.

Getting the most out of life means regularly spending time in reflection, meditation, and reading good books. For these kinds of nourishing activities, it's important to have a peaceful environment that is consistent with your desired state of mind. In a world filled with so much noise and chaos, it's refreshing to have a retreat or oasis.

Consider creating a space with greenery, flowers, and other natural elements. You may even want to add a few inspirational pictures or symbols. I have a room in my home that is overflowing with large plants and flowers. Each morning, I start my day in this room with my morning meditation, followed by a little journal-writing and reading. What a great way to start the day!

If at all possible, try to use a room that allows you to take in the inspiration of the morning sun.

Section 4

Golden Rules

(51)

See Through
the Illusion

*D*ID YOU KNOW that most people are afraid of other people?

I didn't fully realize this until I attended an unusual weekend workshop on personal development. The workshop leader had people who didn't know each other stand approximately one foot (30 centimeters) across from each other and look into each other's eyes. Participants were told not to use social crutches like smiling; they just had to look into each other's eyes and try to connect. We all had a turn doing this.

Then the leader also had 25 members stand up and look at the remaining 75 people. Again our objective was to just to look at other people without any gestures or speech.

I couldn't believe what happened in these two exercises. Approximately one quarter of the group started to cry, another quarter were pretty close to tears, the third quarter showed signs of discomfort, and the rest were fine.

An inflated consciousness is always egocentric and conscious of nothing but its own existence. It is incapable of learning from the past, incapable of understanding contemporary events, and incapable of drawing right conclusions about the future. It is hypnotized by itself and therefore cannot be argued with. It inevitably dooms itself to calamities that must strike it dead.

—Carl Jung,
Swiss psychiatrist

I concluded that most people are so scared of being rejected, of being judged and looking bad, that it's incredibly difficult for them to connect with others.

We're caught up, in various degrees, in the illusion of "looking good," of acting as if we have it all together, of believing that we're separate from each other. The truth is, we're all vulnerable, we all want to feel accepted, and we all want to feel connected.

It's your ego that tells you that you're separate, smarter, richer, dumber, poorer, or just different. As long as you continue to fight the natural laws of being human, your constant shadows in life will be fear, doubt, and anxiety. Only when the ego is tamed will you be able to see through the illusion.

Understand Communication

ONE OF THE GREATEST BOOKS ever written on understanding life is *A Course in Miracles* by Dr. Helen Schucman.

One sentence in the book forever changed the way I listen to and understand people: "All communication is either a loving response or a cry for help."

Think about this for a minute; let it sink in — don't judge it. Understand the wisdom in this simple sentence. Think how this simple truth can enhance your relationships at home, at work, and with yourself.

Seeing the world from this perspective will give you the ability to see through fear, stress, and anxiety to get to the truth.

Everyone wants to be happy, but some people are going about it in the wrong way. Many people don't think about the actions, thoughts, and beliefs that create happiness. Remember this powerful quote any time you're having a conflict with anyone. You'll be more likely to find a solution more quickly and with less stress.

(53)

Be Love

My life is an indivisible whole, and all my attitudes run into one another; and they all have their rise in my insatiable love for mankind.
—Mahatma Gandhi, Indian spiritual and political leader

*T*WO OF THE GREATEST NEEDS of the human soul are to love and be loved.

Even though love is the air and light of our earthly existence, we often ignore its importance. In our quest for success and riches, love is often taken for granted. Sadly, on our deathbed, we come to realize that nothing was ever more important.

Nothing is more important than the love one feels for another, whether it's for a parent, a child, a spouse, or a close friend.

Often the only obstacle to the continuous flow of love in our lives is our ego. Remember, our ego feeds on the need to judge and compare, often criticizing our loved ones. These negative energies prevent us from truly experiencing love. With the absence of love in our life, fear, doubt, and other forms of negative energy can often take root.

So take inventory of your life. Who do you love? Have you told them lately? Don't wait until they're in a hospital bed or a pine box; do it now while you still can! Don't let fear of rejection, pride, or stubbornness prevent you from telling the people who matter most in your life what they really mean to you.

If you need to forgive someone, do it! Are you resenting anyone in your life? Resentment is a poison you are taking; get rid of it.

Once you finally say those three dreaded words (*I love you!*), it will be like the weight of the world was just lifted off your shoulders. You'll feel like you just won the lottery — except this kind of winning is priceless!

54

Stay Away from "Negies"

N EGIES ARE PEOPLE that suck the energy out of you.

You can find negies pretty much everywhere — at work, in your social network, and even in your neighborhood. They can also be found on some of the most popular television programs in America.

At work negies are easiest to identify; they can usually be seen feeding on their favorite food — office gossip. These folks are too busy finding out what everybody else is doing to do any work. They are a very tightknit group in every organization and (thanks to the speed of email) they can spread rumors like wildfire. Motivated by paranoia, they are constantly trying to recruit. *Warning:* They may try to lure you in to their inner circle with "harmless" chat about what happened on *Y & R*, for example. (If you know what these initials stand for, chances are you have already heard too much — run for your life!)

In your social network the negies are not as easy to identify. What will give them away will be their consistent criticism, possibly not of people in your inner circle, but everyone else. They may be prejudiced, judgmental, or closed-minded. Because these negies are your "friends," I suggest you tell them (in as gentle a manner as possible) how offensive you find their negative comments.

In most cases, people don't really want to be negies; it's just a bad habit. Your friends may even thank you for having an interest in their spiritual well-being.

(55)

Tell People How You Feel

I was angry with my friend: I told my wrath, my wrath did end. I was angry with my foe: I told it not, my wrath did grow.

—William Blake, British poet

I BELIEVE one of the biggest reasons we cry at funerals is that we don't fully communicate to our loved ones how much we love them.

Many people let conflicts with friends and family members to remain unresolved out of pride, often for years. Our ego can prevent us from forgiving, healing, and connecting with the people who mean the most to us.

If you have a conflict with a loved one, the simple act of telling that person the result you're hoping to achieve in the relationship is half the battle. This is also the first step to removing the ego from the situation. When that happens, nothing will stand between you and a mutual understanding.

Write down a list of the people who mean the most to you, including family members, friends, associates at work, customers, suppliers, spouses, ex-spouses, and anyone else you can think of. How many of these people know how you feel about them? Next, write down the cost of not communicating how you feel about these people. How do you think your relationships would be affected if you told them?

Beside each name write down what you are committed to doing or saying to let these people know how much they mean to you.

It's quite normal to feel a little awkward about this exercise. After all, we've been conditioned to hide our emotions. Don't let another day go by without letting the people who mean the most to you know how you feel!

56

Don't Compare

**Comparisons are
odious.**
  —Anonymous,
Fourteenth century

*I*T'S OKAY TO COMPARE apples to oranges
or pizza to spaghetti. But comparing
yourself to others prevents you from finding any kind of permanent peace of mind.

The expression "keeping up with the
Joneses" is the best example of comparison
and has become an epidemic in North
America. Many people today use cocktail
parties as a gauge of how they compare to
all the Mr. and Mrs. Joneses they talk to.
"So, where do you live?" "What do you do
for a living?" And, "Where did you go to
school?" These are asked, often unconsciously, to see who is ahead of whom in
the race of life.

Of course, these questions are normal
when you consider that in North America,
our worth as people is calculated based on
those very factors — how much money we
make, who we know, and where we live.
But normal doesn't mean healthy!

One of the main reasons so many people drink excessively or take prescription
drugs for anxiety is to find relief from the

pain of "not measuring up." Happiness, connection with others, and compassion will always elude those who determine their self-worth, and the worth of others, according to external values.

57

Don't Judge

*E*VERY ACT AND THOUGHT you have either creates positive energy or depletes it.

Good deeds, compliments, and genuine acts of kindness create positive energy and momentum in your life.

Many of these positive feelings that we enjoy come from a connection with others. Sometimes it's hard to believe, but we all have a deep desire to connect. Yes, everyone! The need to judge comes from your lower self, or ego, whose only concern is to separate you from people. But judging others will take away your positive energy and disconnect you from others. What's even worse is that it will disconnect you from your source.

Think about it. Next time you judge another person, another culture, or anyone who is "different," catch yourself and pay attention to how you feel at that precise moment. Ten out of ten times you will feel a lower energy in your body. Notice how your judgments rob you of any feelings of peace and goodwill. Being "right" in order to satisfy your ego and justify your judgments just has too high a price.

So guard your thoughts; don't allow another judgment to be spoken from your lips. This will be easier said than done because our culture thrives on judging others. If you watch any popular television programs, listen to any radio programs, or read some of the weekly newsmagazines, you'll see that people are judging each other all the time! The sad thing is that they don't even realize how they are contributing to their own sense of disconnection and misery; they're too caught up in "being right."

Of course, you don't have to agree with everyone. But if internal peace and connection with others is a priority in your life, tolerance must replace judgment.

Practice Tolerance

*I*NTOLERANCE IS LIKE A CLOUD that hangs over your life, blocking the sunshine of kindness, empathy, and compassion.

People have their reasons for harboring prejudices. Some people don't like people with another skin color, different religious beliefs, or conflicting political views. History is full of cultures that have promoted tolerance. Today, the Middle East is rife with intolerance, where all sides have their reasons to hate, based on long histories of bloodshed and upheaval. People there have not come to understand that the enemy they hate is really themselves.

There is a Native American saying: "No tree is foolish enough to fight among its branches." Intolerance is a poison that survives only as long as you believe that you are separate from those you hate. This poison won't necessarily kill you — but it will torment you by attracting misery and blocking the existence of peace in your heart. Remember, we are all connected.

Do you truly want to be wise? Wise people practice tolerance. Tomorrow when you awaken play this game: With all the people that you encounter, look beyond their appearance, beyond their personality, beyond the social mask we all wear. Look into their eyes. Hold eye contact long enough to see into their soul. When you do, the reflection that you see will be you.

When you really, really, really get this, you will never need to read another how-to-build-rapport book again. You will *become* rapport. You will *become* tolerance!

Forgive

*T*O GET THE MOST OUT OF LIFE you must learn to forgive. Until you have done this, true peace of mind, joy, and fulfillment will always be a day away.

Our ego prevents us from forgiving. So many people make the choice, unconsciously, to be "right" rather than to forgive.

Until we forgive, we will continue to bear the weight of the negative emotions, memories, and feelings of the past. These negative energies rob you of your natural enthusiasm and momentum; they will slow you down to a crawl.

The one truth that continues to connect all humanity is that we all want to be happy, loved, and needed. That includes being supported and forgiven.

When we forgive, we open up the channel for positive energies to come back into our life. If you continue to refuse to forgive then you will continue to wear the fate of an unfulfilled life. No amount of pride is worth such a cost.

There is only one thing to do: Call, visit or write anybody and everybody you need to forgive!

Be Compassionate

NO MATTER WHAT your circumstances are, you can find all kinds of opportunity to practice compassion on a daily basis.

Each time you practice compassion you connect to your higher self. Just offering your seat to an older person on the bus is practicing compassion. You can say a silent prayer for a homeless person on your way to work in the morning, or give him or her a hot coffee or a couple of dollars. There's no shortage of opportunities to practice compassion.

With each act of compassion you will feel closer to God, closer to your source, and closer to your true self. Mother Teresa lived for compassion. She was once asked how she could work with the poor in the filth and stench of Calcutta. She responded, "God comes to us in the hungry, the naked, the lonely, the alcoholic, the drug addict, the prostitute, and the street beggars. If we reject them, we reject God himself."

Make it a part of your daily routine — don't put your head on your pillow tonight until you've practiced at least one act of compassion. I can't even begin to explain how good you will feel inside when you adopt this ritual!

Make a Difference

MAKE A DIFFERENCE in someone's life today!

There are so many opportunities for you to offer someone, somewhere, a little encouragement and hope, or just a helping hand. Remember this: It's not what we get in life that makes us happy; it is what we give in life that counts.

If you're like most people, you have approximately 14 to 18 waking hours each day to earn a living, work on your to-do list, and meet the demands of a busy life. Don't let your life go by before you begin to ask one very important daily question: "What did I accomplish today?"

Take a look around your neighborhood. I bet there is a community seniors' home that is looking for a volunteer to play piano on Saturday afternoons. There may be a soup kitchen that could benefit from your dish-washing skills. Or maybe there's a women's shelter that could really use those pillows you don't use.

Every year for about 10 years, I've been

the parade co-coordinator for the Toronto United Way Walkathon. It's not a major time commitment — just one day a year. I get more satisfaction in that one day than I ever imagined I would. I also offer to speak to high school students periodically on getting the most out of life.

It's that easy to make a difference. The spiritual connection that you will get from making a difference gives meaning to your life — and it's extremely addictive!

Think about it — what can you do to make a difference? Better yet, what *will you do* to make a difference?

Do Something Nice (and Don't Tell Anyone)

*P*ERIODICALLY, we find ourselves doing a really good deed for someone.

It may be something as simple as pushing a stranger's car out of the snow, putting a couple of coins in a parking meter so someone doesn't get a ticket, or returning a lost wallet to its rightful owner.

When we find ourselves in these fortunate situations of doing good, it feels incredible! When we do something nice for someone else, we often enjoy a deeper connection to life and a warm feeling inside.

It's tempting to tell others of our heroic deeds. This craving to tell the story of our heroism comes from the ego. The ego is only concerned about making you look good to others. When you surrender to the voice of the ego and tell your story, notice how the act of bragging about your good deed affects that special feeling or connection you got from doing that good deed. What happened to it? It disappeared.

It disappeared because the special

feeling or connection you felt was between you and your source (or spirit or God). It was never between you and your ego.

Remember, your ego weakens you while your spirit strengthens you. Your ego needs to brag while your spirit only needs to rejoice.

Go out and do something nice for someone everyday — and keep it between you and God.

Practice Kindness

*G*ETTING THE MOST OUT OF LIFE is about having a consistent feeling of well-being. It's about connecting with your higher self.

There is no better way of finding this peace of mind than by practicing kindness. The act of kindness produces serotonin in the brain, which creates a feeling of well-being. It also strengthens your body's immune system.

Amazingly, both the receiver and the giver of an act of kindness experience an increase in serotonin levels. Even a witness to an act of kindness receives an increase in serotonin levels.

But don't take my word for it; see for yourself. Go out and be kind to someone — preferably a stranger — and notice what happens. You don't have to save the world; just do something nice for someone. If you see someone struggling to open a door, offer to help; if you see someone puzzling over a map (and who hasn't), offer your assistance.

Each act of kindness increases your reservoir of well-being and connection. There are a zillion acts of kindness you can do in your lifetime, so start today!

64

Say Please and Thank You

A s I mentioned earlier, we all share a common desire for connection.

Connection with other people makes the world seem smaller, kinder, and more full of love. There is no commodity more valuable than connection.

Every day we are surrounded with opportunities to connect with other people simply by being courteous. People underestimate the power of a kind word, which, if spoken with sincerity, can take down the biggest barriers.

In my experience, whether I say "please" or "thank you," I usually receive a kind acknowledgement as well as a smile. Courtesy opens doors (pun intended!) and nurtures friendships.

The simple habit of courtesy will elevate your consciousness and all those you come in contact with in a particular moment.

Saying please and thank you will create goodwill in your world. This goodwill will radiate from the core of your soul and give your life meaning and value. So make it your mission to be an ambassador of goodwill.

65

Serve Others

S OONER OR LATER we realize that one of the purest forms of joy is found in the act of serving others. When we focus on the needs of others, our ego temporarily loses its voice.

What do you do for a living? No matter what the answer (even if you're retired), you probably serve someone or something. Creating more joy in life can be found in giving more service or giving a higher level of service. Are you currently giving one hundred per cent at work? Are you as prompt, efficient, organized, courteous, and enthusiastic as you can be? Or do you have limiting self-talk like, "They don't pay me enough to give one hundred per cent?" Many people unconsciously have this kind of voice in their minds.

Make a list of five duties you perform in your job to serve your clients, boss, or organization. Beside each duty, write down three small activities you could do to add value to each duty. For example, you may have listed customer service as one of

Consciously or unconsciously, every one of us does render some service or other. If we cultivate the habit of doing this service deliberately, our desire for service will steadily grow stronger and will make not only our own happiness, but that of the world at large.
—Mahatma Gandhi,
Indian spiritual and
political leader

your duties. Sending birthday cards or annual customer satisfaction question-naires, or organizing client-appreciation events are a few ideas to get you started.

Always Keep Your Word

Your life works to the degree you keep your agreements.
—Warner Erhard, American entrepreneur

WHEN OUR WORD IS OUR BOND we become someone people count on.

When our word is our agreement we are living with integrity. To be consistent in thought, as well as in action, is to live with the purest of intentions.

People who live with integrity are given the most responsibility in life and, ultimately, the highest rewards.

Today, our word has been replaced in most places by our signature. Collectively, our word has come to mean very little.

But when we don't keep our word we lose our self-confidence, self-respect, and passion for living. Think about this for a minute: How would your life be affected today if you kept your word one hundred per cent of the time? How would this small adjustment in your actions affect your monthly commitments? Would you be more likely to accomplish your goals and stick to your plan? Would you be less likely to make commitments that are inconsistent with your values?

Write Thank-You Cards

S END A MINIMUM of one thank-you card each week.

This activity nurtures your spirit, builds goodwill in your relationships, and teaches you to focus on gratitude.

Keep a list of the people you send cards to — not to keep score or to figure out who owes you a card, but so that you know how many people you have to be grateful for.

This exercise alone will create a feeling of wealth that is recession-proof, never loses value, and compounds at an astronomical rate.

Go out and get a gratitude journal. Make a list of all the people you want to send a thank-you card to. Think of friends you have had for years. Don't forget about all the friends who have ever helped you move — these are the truest of friends.

Send thank-you cards to people who have taught you lessons in life (usually these are people who really annoyed you at one time).

At first, people will think you're dying — and you are! Remember, life is terminal. If you remember that little fact, you'll be less likely to let your ego get in the way and more likely to send someone a thank-you card!

68

Give Compliments

MARY KAY ASH, of Mary Kay Cosmetics, used to say: "Pretend that every single person that you meet has a sign around their head that says: 'Make me feel important.' Not only will you succeed in sales, you'll succeed in life."

We all know how good it feels when someone unexpectedly says something nice to us about our appearance, our efforts, or our personality. It feels terrific!

Nothing strengthens relationships like sincere appreciation for each other. Nothing breaks the ice with a stranger like a sincere compliment does; it makes all kinds of barriers melt.

Think about how many people serve you in one way or another every day — the dry cleaner, the pizza delivery man, and the woman at the drive-through coffee shop. Be appreciative of everything that comes your way today and pay for it in compliments. To the dry cleaner say, "I sure appreciate how clean you get my shirts." To the pizza delivery man, say,

"Thanks for getting here so fast." And to the woman at the drive-through coffee shop say, "You make the best coffee I've ever had." Don't underestimate these seemingly insignificant acts of kindness because they create miracles.

People often hold back giving compliments for a variety of reasons, none of which are any good. Why withhold sunshine?

So look around and see who deserves a compliment or two in your life — you'll be glad you did!

Talk to Strangers

Don't be afraid of
showing affection.
Be warm and
tender, thoughtful
and affectionate.
—Sir John Lubbock,
British statesman

*I*F YOU LIVE IN A SMALL TOWN, you can skip this one. This is for those of us who live in the urban jungles of the world. We have become experts at ignoring people. We ignore people beside us on the bus, in line at the bank, and in countless other everyday situations. You're not supposed to talk to strangers — they're strange.

Well, if you're not supposed to talk to strangers how are you ever going to meet anyone? I don't know who made up this silly rule but it's absolutely crazy! There are no strangers. There is just the *illusion* of a stranger. The illusion disappears when sincere greetings are exchanged.

Each time we meet a stranger and smiles are exchanged, for a brief moment we connect to the place that makes us one, to the place that reaffirms that there are no strangers.

Each day grants you countless opportunities to speak to strangers. They're everywhere! They're on the street, at restaurants, at business functions — and most of them want to talk to you.

Have you ever been in an elevator with only one other person? Usually a polite nod is exchanged — but if you attempt a little chit-chat, in my experience you'll get pleasant chit-chat right back about nine out of ten times. And you'll usually feel a sense of connection during and after the chit-chat, not just with that person but also with your source.

Remember, each time we meet a stranger and exchange pleasantries, we make the world a little smaller and a whole lot warmer!

Section 5

Keeping the Balance

Be Spontaneous

*T*O GET THE MOST OUT OF LIFE you need to set goals, plan, and prepare for the life that you want to create for yourself.

The danger, however, in being too goal-oriented is becoming inflexible. You need to remember that some of the best moments in your life will be unexpected.

Take a few moments now to reflect on your life — isn't it true that some of the most memorable moments were created out of spontaneity?

Spontaneity creates an explosion that, for that moment, frees you to create a new experience outside the realm of the known — the type of unexpected adventure that makes life exciting and fresh. Without spontaneity, your life becomes a prison of memories, routines, and boredom.

Consider your goals a roadmap for your journey in life, but be open to all the wonderful side trails that aren't on your map. Sometimes you'll find shortcuts and other times you'll stumble across a breath-taking view!

Smile

A smile cures the wounding of a frown.

—William Shakespeare

*T*HE WORLD IS FAR TOO SERIOUS and we, in turn, take ourselves far too seriously. Remember that life is meant to be enjoyed.

Have you ever watched people being too serious? I see them all the time at the grocery store, in traffic, or waiting in line. In the grocery store, I often overhear people on their cell phones reporting back to base camp: "I got the milk and I'll be home in 17 minutes."

Grocery store line-ups are among the best places to observe people being serious, especially if the line is not moving very fast. When you notice yourself being one of these serious people in the line-up, snap out of it! Look around with untamed curiosity. Notice how wonderful this moment is, or could be. Notice other people's grocery carts. Ask the person behind you if her brand of soup is any good. Watch the curious three-year-old two rows down trying to reach for the candy by the cashier.

Don't make the mistake of letting an opportunity to be with people and enjoy "just being alive" pass you by.

And finally, *smile.* Did you know that when we smile our body releases endorphins? Next time you're in line at the bank or grocery store or wherever, smile at someone. Smiling is one of the greatest ways to release tension and break down barriers.

Never underestimate the impact of a smile. When a smile is returned, it means the *divinity* in you just connected to the *divinity* in another, and this is magic!

(72)

Get Excited About Your Life

Being excited about something or someone or somewhere is what life is all about. Look for reasons to be excited. You're surrounded by them.
—Derrick Sweet, Motivational/ Inspirational speaker and author of *Get the Most Out of Life*

M ANY PEOPLE look outside their own life for excitement.

Sadly, these people often see more excitement in the lives of fictional characters (Agent 007 or even Scooby Doo) than they could ever imagine in their own humdrum existence.

It's true that, as a society, we've been conditioned to count on Hollywood for a large portion of our collective excitement. We've become accustomed to watching rather than creating excitement in our lives. We have been sold on the idea that being a spectator is good. Is it any wonder obesity is rapidly becoming the norm in our society?

The only kind of excitement that exhilarates the soul — I mean, right down to its core — is the kind of excitement that *you* create, the kind that *you* experience — live and in person!

So make a list of what gets you so excited you can't sleep! Come up with a list of 20 things that you could go out and do, right now, to create excitement in your life. Have you ever considered mountain-biking, skiing, sailing, or learning how to make sushi?

You may even find it exciting to quit your job (only if it bores you silly) and do something that you've always dreamed of. That could be exciting!

You may consider learning a new language, taking up a martial art, or joining a public speaking organization like Toastmasters to create more excitement in your life.

Make your list now. Don't read another page — do it now!

Be Outrageous

M EDIOCRITY has become an epidemic. Life, for many, is made up of a series of daily mundane redundancies.

For most people, life is about getting up at 6 a.m., skipping a nutritious breakfast, going to work till 5 p.m., coming home to do a few chores, eating dinner, escaping reality for a few hours via bad television, having 11 minutes of meaningless chit-chat with their loved ones, and then repeating the whole thing over again tomorrow and the next day and the next. If humankind has a universal theme today it's, "Why bother?"

To get the most out of life today you need to be outrageous! When we find ourselves having moments of outrageousness we are alive in the truest sense of the word.

To be outrageous is to be extreme with your passions, to not hold back your enthusiasm when your spirits are high.

You have these moments from time to time — when the world seems to be beating to your pulse and everything is working as it should. Being outrageous means having more of these moments; it means being able to find significance in a world that is focused on insignificance.

Being outrageous means refusing to settle for anything less than your heart's desire. It means listening to your heart when it tells you to give "that homeless guy" (the guy that you've walked past a zillion times) a crispy 20-dollar bill.

It means that you actually believe you can make a difference in the world by all the seemingly insignificant acts of kindness that you give to the world.

It means that the world just may be a better place because of your being here. It's your choice!

(74)

Write Down 100 Things You Want to Do Before You Die

*T*HINK BACK to when you were a little kid. If you were like most kids you probably talked about all the amazing things you would do when you grew up.

Have you turned some of these dreams into reality yet? What kind of promises did you make to yourself that are still unfulfilled? What kind of hobbies did you see yourself pursuing that have yet to be pursued? Even now, what outrageous things do you still want to do? Have you considered sky-diving, running a marathon, or scuba-diving?

Think about this question as it applies to your work, relationships, and personal goals. Think about the places you want to visit, the experiences you want to have, and the contributions you would like to make.

Find a blank hardcover notebook and write down one hundred things you want to do before you die. Give your book a title: *One Hundred Things I'm Going to Do Before I Die*. Write the title of each activity at the top of a page, and leave the rest of the page blank.

After you finish writing your list of one hundred, take a few minutes to review it. Prioritize your list using the ABC system we saw in "Honor Your Values" (chapter 19), where the "As" are the top priorities, "Bs" are second, and "Cs" are third.

Once you've finished separating your priorities into three categories, go back and rank each activity according to importance to you. For example, A1 is more important than A3, which is more important than B1.

Finally, assign a due date for each item and write any steps or plans that may be necessary to make each activity happen.

Make sure you leave enough room for comments on how you feel after you accomplish each activity. What a legacy this will be!

Have fun with this exercise. Get excited about this exercise! But most of all, *do this exercise!* I promise it will be one of the greatest tools you'll have to help you get the most out of life.

Practice the "One-Time-Only" Formula

MANY OF THE LATEST self-improvement and spiritual books talk about the importance of "living in the moment."

Few, however, offer advice on how to actually begin.

So, how do you start? You have to work at it. Anytime you catch yourself daydreaming in a meeting, not giving your full attention to a conversation, or worrying about what didn't happen yesterday or what could happen tomorrow, *catch yourself!* Put yourself back in the moment.

Remember, this takes discipline. The good news is that once you're aware of this process it does gradually get easier.

In the meantime here's an exercise to teach you how to start living in the moment. *Caution*: Only do this exercise when you don't have any immediate major commitments! Tomorrow, when you wake up, pretend that this will be the first time and the last time, in fact, the *only* time, that you will ever be alive.

For maximum results apply one hundred per cent of your imagination to this exercise. This will be hard to do the first time because we are so used to taking life for granted.

You will notice that food has a richer taste, air actually has a taste, and the sunrise is a magnificent event that happens every single day! You may even find yourself making bold statements like: "My wife is a Goddess!" or "All my problems have been little more than an illusion created by the same powerful imagination that is making this one-time-only formula such an *eye-opener!*"

Enough said. Do the exercise!

Bark Like a Dog

The great pleasure of a dog is that you may make a fool of yourself with him and not only will he not scold you, but he will make a fool of himself too.
—Samuel Butler, British writer

DO YOU HAVE A DOG, or have a friend who has a dog?

My wife Marsha and I have two dogs, Sadie and Numan. Dogs don't just accept people, they love people. They realize how counter-productive it is to their "puppy outlook" to judge, criticize, or complain. They just want to be happy, like we humans — but they're better at it.

I've learned a lot about life from our dogs and have come to admire their outlook. Dogs are always happy to see you. The first thing they do when they see you coming in the front door is wag their tail. It's like they're saying, "Good to see ya, where ya been, good to see ya, where ya been, let's play." Humans should try this.

Dogs are enthusiastic most of the time. If I suggest that we go for a walk or have a snack they go berserk. Could you imagine how much fun it would be to hang out with a human who was like this?

Dogs only know how to live in the moment; they're not caught up thinking about the fire hydrant that they didn't pee on last week, or the remark I made two weeks ago about their breath or the French poodle that hasn't been to the park in a month. They truly live in the here and now. Maybe they're born with an intuitive understanding that they're only here for a short time and there is no time to waste.

I also admire the fact that they don't take themselves too seriously. People could learn a thing or two from dogs.

Pick a Theme Song for Your Life

Music is the mediator between the spiritual and the sensual life.
—Ludwig Van Beethoven, German composer

*A*S WE'VE ALREADY SEEN, music is one of the most powerful tools for elevating your emotions.

Movie producers use music to create mood and make us cry, laugh, or be fearful. Advertisers use music to motivate us to purchase products. We can also use music to inspire ourselves to be our best.

If you had to pick a song that illustrated the theme to your life, what would it be? Perhaps you would choose Louis Armstrong's "What a Wonderful World," or maybe you would prefer Frank Sinatra's "When You're Smiling (The Whole World Smiles with You)."

Motivational speaker Loretta LaRoche, one of the most powerful speakers I have ever heard, uses the theme to Mighty Mouse as one of her theme songs. Loretta can often be heard across America singing: "Here I come to save the day!"

Music can be used as a tool to produce the emotions we want in order to perform at our best. One of my favorite motivational theme songs is Bill Conti's theme from Rocky, "Gonna Fly Now."

Think of a song or group of songs that inspires you. Play these songs when you're exercising, writing your goals, or visualizing yourself creating your future. Play your theme song before a big meeting or sales presentation. The added emotional boost from your theme song will create a feeling of inspiration that will fuel your ascent.

You may even want to use your theme song as background music for your self-commercial exercise (see "Write Your Own Commercial", chapter 11).

(78)

Be Grateful

Gratitude is not only the greatest of virtues, but the parent of all others.
—Marcus T. Cicero, Roman orator

*G*RATITUDE turns an ordinary moment into a celebration, a meal into a feast, a home into a castle, and a disappointment into a lesson.

When you practice gratitude, not only do you experience a feeling of complete abundance, but more abundance will be attracted to you in all areas of your life. This is the universal law of attraction, as described in "Meditate" in chapter 36.

In a world that values the illusion that more is better, gratitude and the real feeling of wealth are seldom attained. Most people are too busy chasing the next goal to appreciate all the completed goals of the past. They're too busy focusing on what they want to enjoy what they already have. This "poverty mentality" eventually creates a feeling of emptiness.

Remember, usually too late in life we realize that the "little things" (watching the sun rise, receiving a sincere smile, and connecting with people) are really the big things and the "big things" (recognition from your peers, the stuff that you just had to have) were really the little things.

Practice gratitude every day. Tomorrow when you wake up, and every morning after, ask yourself, "What do I have to be grateful for?"

Nurture Yourself

Every one of us need to show how much we care for each other, and in the process, care for ourselves.
—Diana, Princess of Wales

*A*s we saw in section 4, "Golden Rules," life is pretty much meaningless without relationships.

Your relationships with your family, friends, and associates need to be the best they can be.

But your relationship with yourself is the most important relationship you will ever have. Who else knows all your deepest hopes, fears, and ambitions?

What kind of relationship do you have with yourself? Are you good to yourself? What does your self-talk sound like? Do you say things like: "Things are going to work out just fine"? Or is your self-talk defeatist?

You must be your biggest fan. This has nothing to do with arrogance; it is about making peace with yourself, accepting yourself, and loving yourself. Only when you love yourself are you able to have nurturing relationships with others.

All the gifts of appreciation, gratitude, and affection must be felt inwards before they can be sincerely expressed outwards. Be good to yourself. Pamper yourself with a trip to the spa, have a manicure, take yourself out to lunch, sleep late one Sunday morning.

Do anything that comes to mind that will nurture your relationship with yourself.

Act Like a Baby

*H*AVE YOU EVER NOTICED how people react when they see a baby?

They stop everything, smile from ear to ear, and, in a cheerful voice, say something like: "And how are you today?" or "You are soooo beautiful!" or "Can I take you home with me?"

Why is that? It's because babies are vulnerable, and they have no choice but to show it. Puppies too. We love vulnerability! We love being around anybody and anything that shows vulnerability.

As we get older, we are less vulnerable — we become independent, form opinions about our world, and develop a thick skin to protect us from "verbal torpedoes." We learn to become judgmental, opinionated, critical, and even (at times) mean-spirited. Would you want to hold a baby who fits this description?

Babies are nothing but pure bliss because they haven't been taught (yet) to judge, hate, or complain. Babies accept everybody and maybe that's why we don't hesitate to give them our best. We know we will not be rejected.

So, camp out in the diaper aisle at your local grocery store for a while. Observe a few of these little titans of tenderness, or better yet, offer your baby-sitting services to your friends and relatives. It will give you a great opportunity to catch up on some essential skills for getting the most out of life!

(81)

Be Unrealistic

WHEN I WAS A TEENAGER things weren't too good. I hated school, life, and myself. I was going nowhere fast.

By the time I was 16 I was a high school drop-out, a big fan of marijuana, and I had a mouth that made Ozzy Osborne sound like Shirley Temple. My only ambitions were to hitch-hike across Canada, watch television, and get high.

It would have been realistic for my parents, Betty and Ray, not to expect little Derrick Sweet to amount to much. Fortunately for me, my parents were unrealistic.

Being unrealistic means not accepting the status quo. At one time it was considered unrealistic to run a mile in under four minutes, perform corrective eye surgery, or fly from New York to London in less than four hours.

And given my behavior, it was pretty unrealistic to expect little Derrick Sweet to live up to his potential.

But my parents saw something in me

that no one else did. In their mind's eye, they could see who I really was and what I was capable of achieving.

Twenty-two years ago, if you were to say to people who knew me that I would go back to high school, graduate with a B.A. in Business from Johnson State in Vermont, own several businesses, become a financial advisor and manage close to $60 million, then retire from the distinguished position of Vice President (Senior Investment Advisor) with one of the largest investment firms in Canada at age 38, become a writer, motivational speaker, and founder, chairman, and CEO of one of the most exciting personal development companies in the world, they would have said these things were totally unrealistic.

But my parents believed in me. I will always be grateful to have been brought up by such unrealistic people.

What do you have to be unrealistic about? What dreams have you been putting off because they're too unrealistic? Take out your pen and write anything that comes to mind — about your career, your health, your relationships, and any other area of your life that needs a tune-up.

Be Enthusiastic

Enthusiasm is the yeast that makes your hopes shine to the stars. Enthusiasm is the sparkle in your eyes, the swing in your gait. The grip of your hand, the irresistible surge of will and energy to execute your ideas.

—Henry Ford, Founder of the Ford Motor Company

ENTHUSIASM, gusto, zeal, eagerness, and passion describe pretty much the same thing — a highly desirably and seldom enjoyed feeling of being alive in the largest capacity.

To have a bodacious appetite for life is to be enthusiastic. Good things happen to enthusiastic people; business and social opportunities abound for those in this state of mind.

Being enthusiastic is easy when you know where you're going in life, when your goals are clearly defined, and you're living your purpose.

Sure, it is impossible to be enthusiastic all the time. And sometimes you'll need to be enthusiastic for an important meeting or presentation even if you don't feel like it. The masters in life realize that if you just act enthusiastic, before long you'll feel that way.

How would an enthusiastic person carry him- or herself? They would most likely sit or stand erect (no slouching!).

How would they speak? They would probably be upbeat and have a positive tone in their voice.

Try those for starters and before you know it you'll feel — and want to remain — enthusiastic.

Laugh

DO YOU REMEMBER how much you laughed when you were a child?

Children often laugh as much as 400 times a day, whereas most adults are lucky to laugh a dozen times a day.

I believe our true nature is to have fun and to laugh. We all have a little fool inside us who just wants to experience the joy of laughter.

When we laugh, our bodies release endorphins, the body's natural upper. When you laugh so hard that your eyes water, you release a healing enzyme. Did you know that laughter prevents colds and respiratory viruses?

Laughter has been known to reduce blood pressure, aid in digestion, and even heal the soul.

In business meetings, laughter cuts through tension and helps build rapport.

Spend time with people who share your sense of humor; go see a funny movie or visit a comedy club. Remember that without laughter, life is boring.

Look for every opportunity to laugh because when you're laughing, the whole world really does laugh with you!

(84)

Watch
Funny Movies

Laughter is the shortest distance between two people.
—Victor Borge, Danish entertainer

NORMAN COUSINS' doctors told him he had six months to live.

They told him that there was a one-in-five-hundred chance of beating his disease. In *Anatomy of an Illness,* Cousins shares his experience of using laughter as medicine. He decided to use what life he had left to experiment by watching funny movies, reading comic material, telling and listening to jokes.

He was in constant pain but laughing for only five minutes reduced the pain enough for him to sleep many hours.

Cousins survived his illness. And his book, in print for over 25 years, is regarded as a must-read in the medical community.

One of the simplest but most satisfying pleasures in life is to be happy. Funny movies or television programs are among the easiest ways to "get happy." I wholeheartedly recommend you hire Eddie Murphy, Bill Cosby, Chris Rock, Dana Carvey, and Jim Carrey. Have a weekly

appointment with these guys. They're all waiting for you at your local video store.

Remember, we don't laugh because we're happy, we're happy because we laugh!

Section 6

Last Remarks

Review this Book

E VERY NOW AND THEN I hear or see an advertisement for a company using the slogan, "Knowledge is power." Nothing could be further from the truth.

Knowledge isn't power, it's *potential* power. Power is only achieved through putting knowledge to work by taking action.

Some people are going to read this book, be inspired, maybe even "moved," and then they're going to continue to do what they've always done and get what they've always gotten out of life. They're going to get back into their familiar routine in a matter of days or weeks.

You probably made it this far with my book because you sincerely do want, and believe it's possible, to get the most out of life. Again, to get the most out of life today, you need to take action.

Your first action to take is to re-read this book. There's enough wisdom in this book to guide you through one hundred successful lifetimes. If you study, memorize, and teach the life-empowering principles in this book, you will notice a gradual evolution of your spirit and your potential. Eventually you'll arrive at a place within your spirit where there are no limitations; don't be intimidated by that place! Remember to use this power with pure intention — abuse it for selfish or ill intentions and it will leave you.

Review this book on a quarterly basis; it will serve not only as the map to your destiny, but also as your compass. Review this book when you're feeling victorious and review it when you're feeling down.

And remember, the principles contained in this book are pure, simple, proven, and time-tested by the likes of Buddha, Aristotle, Abraham Lincoln, Helen Keller, Eleanor Roosevelt, Marcus Aurelius, and so many others who got the most out of their life.

Good luck and God bless!

Now — Get Started!

*J*UST SO YOU AREN'T TEMPTED to put down this book and have it disappear into your bookshelf, here is a place to begin.

Get out your journal and write down the following statements, each at the top of its own page. Then make a list of answers for each of them — you don't have to do this all at once, but come back to it!

After you've filled each page, reflect on your answers. Then prioritize them as we've talked about before.

Finally, make some due dates.

Go, now! Get your notebook and get going!

1. I love my life because...

2. What I'm looking forward to most for the next 20 years is...

3. From this day forward I will get the most out of life by...

4. The most important goal in my life is...

5a. The people who mean the most to me are...

5b. This is how I will show them...

6a. These are the fears, doubts, and anxieties that have held me back...

6b. Today I will release them by...

7. Each morning when I awaken I'm grateful for...

8. These are the ways that I will offer my kindness to the world....

9. The world is a better place for having me because I...

10a. The negative thoughts that weaken me are...

10b. The positive thought to replace this false programming is...

11. I will be remembered most for...

About the Author

Derrick Sweet is the founder and chairman of the Healthy Wealthy and Wise Corporation, a progressive international human development company that specializes in life improvement seminars and keynote speeches.

Derrick travels extensively, speaking to leading corporations, government organizations, and major associations about the true meaning of wealth, as it applies to the mind, body, and soul.

Derrick's previous work, *Healthy Wealthy and Wise: The Common Sense Guide to Creating Abundance in Life* has been highly acclaimed.

Prior to founding the Healthy Wealthy and Wise Corporation, Derrick worked in the financial services industry. Before retiring at age 38 from his position as Vice President and Senior Investment Advisor at one of the largest investment firms in Canada, Derrick managed approximately $60 million for clients in Canada, Ireland, Spain, Japan, and Australia.

Derrick has a B.A. from Johnson State, in Johnson, Vermont. He lives in Toronto, Canada, with his wife Marsha. To learn more about the Healthy Wealthy and Wise Corporation please visit healthywealthyandwise.com or call toll-free (from Canada and the United States) 1-866-455-2155.

About the Healthy Wealthy and Wise® Corporation

Seminar / Keynote Speech Division

The Seminar/Keynote Speech Division specializes in life improvement seminars and keynote speeches. Our mission is to teach leading corporations, government organizations and major associations about the true meaning of wealth as it applies to the mind, body and soul. We educate our clients on strategies that will allow them to create more joy, peace of mind and prosperity in all the important areas of a well balanced life. We are especially renowned for our Get the Most Out of Life presentations (based on Derrick Sweet's book of the same name) where we teach our clients all the "little" things we can do everyday to live with more passion, purpose and contribution! Our speakers and trainers are all personally trained by Derrick Sweet. For more information please call 1-866-455-2155 or visit www.healthywealthyandwise.com.

Wealth Creation Division

The Healthy Wealthy and Wise® Corporation offers a very unique business opportunity for individuals seeking to work part- or full-time in an environment where they can promote, market and distribute the best information on topics related to health, wealth and wisdom, including: fitness, exercise, diet, investing, retirement planning, tax-reduction strategies, time management, goal-setting techniques, relationships, motivation and inspiration. We offer an attractive commission-based compensation package for individuals who are seeking an opportunity with a progressive, fun and exciting wealth creation corporation. For more information please call Derrick at 1-866-455-2155, email him at dsweet@healthywealthyandwise or visit www.wealthcreationprogram.com.

We Would Love to Hear from You!

Derrick Sweet would love to hear how *Get the Most Out of Life* has affected your day-to-day activities, your habits and your outlook on life.

Do you have an interesting story that resulted from something you read or tried from this book? Please email your story to

dsweet@healthywealthyandwise.com

or write to:

Derrick Sweet
c/o The Healthy Wealthy and Wise Corporation
1 Yonge Street, Suite 1801
Toronto, Ontario
M5E 1W7 Canada

If we use your story in our newsletter we will send you an official "Get the Most Out of Life" T-shirt or baseball cap.

Get the Most Out
of Your Next Event!

Derrick Sweet is known as a truly gifted speaker. He speaks from his heart on what we can all do to live in the realm of our higher self, create internal wealth, make a significant contribution, live with a greater sense of purpose and truly Get the Most Out of Life! His hearty laugh, sense of humor and ability to inspire his audiences to new heights are distinct trademarks of an unforgettable experience with Derrick Sweet. To find out why Derrick's presentations are in high demand by Fortune-500 companies, major financial institutions, large associations and government agencies please call David Aaron at 1-866-455-2155 or email him at info@healthywealthyandwise.com

Derrick Sweet is a truly wonderful individual; a positive outlook, humor and enthusiasm are of utmost importance in life and Derrick exudes these qualities in the presentation; his synergy with the participants is amazing! His integrity and authenticity are refreshing. His hands-on approach was simple to understand and easy to integrate into one's daily life. His ideas help us focus on our goals and develop a new way of seeing life.

—François Duguay
Learning Centre administrator,
Rogers Communications Inc.

Look for these other great Warwick books at your favorite bookstore:

Feng Shui for Business & Office
Cutting-Edge Knowledge from Feng Shui Wisdom
Dr. Jes T.Y. Lim

World-renowned Feng Shui consultant Dr. Jes T. Y. Lim reveals how you can use this ancient practice to improve the health of your business and the wellness of your employees. ISBN 1-894622-24-3

The Vegetarian Traveler
A guide to eating green in 197 countries
Bryan Geon

Vegetarians and people who wish to avoid eating meat for health reasons when traveling often encounter linguistic and cultural barriers on the road. *The Vegetarian Traveler* is the first guide to the words and phrases needed to order vegetarian foods in over 200 countries and territories. World traveler and long-time vegetarian Bryan Geon also gives informative and witty insights into what to expect when attempting to order meatless meals around the world. ISBN 1-894020-85-5

How to Survive Without a Salary
Learning how to live the Conserver Lifestyle
Charles Long

Too many of us trade our happiness and well-being for the reliability of a steady paycheck. Is there any way out of this dilemma? Charles Long offers one possibility — the Conserver Lifestyle. Long shows you how to reduce your cash needs to a level you can easily meet with casual income so that you can live the life you've always dreamed of. This is not a dreary tome about budgeting, however — Long draws on his own family's decades of livng without a salary for amusing anecdotes that confirm conserving as a joyful, liberating way to live.
ISBN 1-894622-37-5

Please visit our website, www.warwickgp.com, for more information about our books.